Aikido

Aikido

PETER BRADY | DEVELOP MIND AND BODY WITH GRACEFUL
AND POWERFUL DEFENCE TECHNIQUES

POSTURES, MOVEMENTS, PINS, FALLS,
THROWS, AND SOLO AND PAIRED
EXERCISES ARE CLEARLY DEMONSTRATED
STEP-BY-STEP IN MORE THAN 500
PHOTOGRAPHS

PHOTOGRAPHY BY MIKE JAMES

LORENZ BOOKS

Dedication
To Mr William Smith MBE – for his leadership, dedication, dignity, integrity
and friendship.

This edition is published by Lorenz Books

Lorenz Books is an imprint of Anness Publishing Ltd
Hermes House, 88–89 Blackfriars Road, London SE1 8HA
tel. 020 7401 2077; fax 020 7633 9499
www.lorenzbooks.com; www.annesspublishing.com

If you like the images in this book and would like to investigate using them
for publishing, promotions or advertising, please visit our website
www.practicalpictures.com for more information.

© Anness Publishing Ltd 2006

UK agent: The Manning Partnership Ltd, 6 The Old Dairy,
Melcombe Road, Bath BA2 3LR; tel. 01225 478 444;
fax 01225 478 440; sales@manning-partnership.co.uk

UK distributor: Grantham Book Services Ltd, Isaac Newton Way,
Alma Park Industrial Estate, Grantham, Lincs NG31 9SD;
tel. 01476 541080; fax 01476 541061; orders@gbs.tbs-ltd.co.uk

North American agent/distributor: National Book Network,
4501 Forbes Boulevard, Suite 200, Lanham, MD 20706;
tel. 301 459 3366; fax 301 429 5746; www.nbnbooks.com

Australian agent/distributor: Pan Macmillan Australia, Level 18,
St Martins Tower, 31 Market St, Sydney, NSW 2000;
tel. 1300 135 113; fax 1300 135 103; customer.service@macmillan.com.au

New Zealand agent/distributor: David Bateman Ltd, 30 Tarndale Grove,
Off Bush Road, Albany, Auckland; tel. (09) 415 7664; fax (09) 415 8892

A CIP catalogue record for this book is available from the British Library.

Publisher Joanna Lorenz; **Editorial Director** Judith Simons;
Project Editors Doreen Gillon and Emma Clegg; **Editorial Reader**
Jay Thundercliffe; **Designer** Lisa Tai; **Photography** Mike James;
Models: Kevin Beggan, Charlotte Brady, James Brady, Jonathan Brady,
Peter Brady, Cath Davis, Rivington Hermitt, Richard Hughes, Paul Jarvis,
Eddie McCalla, Kelly Magna, Neil Mould, Clifford Price, Bryn Ross and
Debbie Shadbolt; **Production Controller** Claire Rae

The author and publishers have made every effort to ensure that all
instructions contained within this book are accurate and safe, and cannot
accept liability for any resulting injury, damage or loss to persons or
property, however it may arise. If you do have any special needs or problems,
consult a doctor or other qualified professional. This book cannot replace
medical consultation and should be used in conjunction with professional
advice. You should not attempt aikido without training from a properly
qualified practitioner.

10 9 8 7 6 5 4 3 2 1

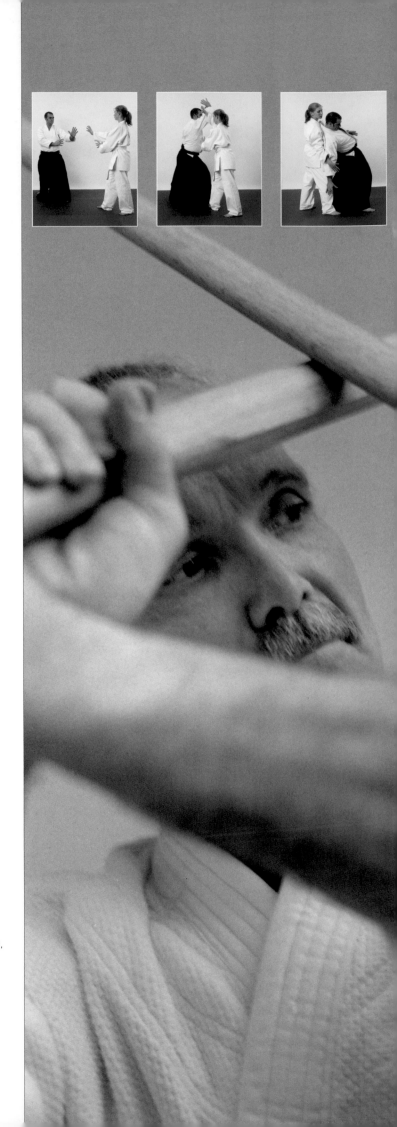

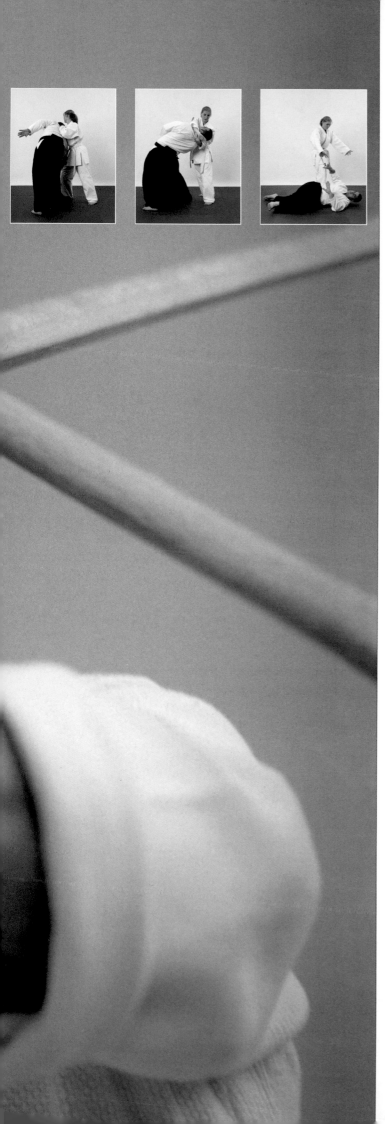

Contents

Introduction

Aikido is a Japanese martial practice that operates on many different levels. At a basic level it teaches that you can overcome an aggressive attack by harmonizing with it, as opposed to meeting force with force. The defensive movements are designed to blend with an attack, lead it until neutralized and then apply a controlling technique. You learn to apply pinning, locking and throwing movements and combinations of these against any attack.

The strategies of defence are drawn from several of the classical martial arts of Japan, such as jujutsu (grappling), kenjutsu (swordsmanship) and yari jutsu (spearfighting) and, when coupled with the aikido founder Morihei Ueshiba's concept of "aiki" (way of harmonizing the spirit), the techniques crystallize into powerful linear, circular and spiral movements that are beautiful to watch, but devastatingly effective when applied.

People usually start aikido in order to learn something of self-defence, improve their physical fitness or learn a little about Japanese culture. People also tend to be drawn to aikido because of its spiritual dimension – among other benefits, it is possible to apply the philosophy of the practice to bring about a more fulfilling quality of life. At its highest level, aikido becomes a vehicle for physical and spiritual integration to a degree that individuals can clearly see themselves as being at one with humanity, nature and the universe itself. When you go to a dojo, or training hall,

Below Chiba Sensei in action at the United Kingdom Aikikai Summer School at Birmingham University, August 1988.

for the first time you embark on a journey that will take you through all the standards of, and approaches to aikido, as long as the individual commitment is there.

BENEFITS OF AIKIDO TRAINING

When looking for ways to become physically fit, most people think in terms of their local gym or leisure centre. Some people consider swimming, dancing or step-aerobics classes; some recognize that they need to build up their strength, so enrol at a local weight-training facility; others may need more stamina, and so join a running club. As a means to an end, there is nothing wrong with any of these disciplines. And while they will yield the desired results if approached with commitment, some people may feel that they need a sense of direction, something to occupy their mind as well as their body.

Unfortunately, training in aikido, or in any of the martial arts for that matter, does not immediately spring to most people's mind when considering a physical-training regime. Many have a misguided impression that the martial arts are only for those who want to dominate or control others or to inflict pain. In fact, quite the opposite is true. As you learn the many throws, pins and projections, it becomes evident that their execution actually promotes health. There is no fighting with your partner, no trying to beat him or her; there is only a harmonious blending of movement that results in a feeling of exhilaration and self-control. If the instructor has taught the concept of ukemi properly – this is the art of learning to fall safely – when you leave the dojo you should feel as if you have had your whole body gently stretched and massaged.

A NON-VIOLENT PRACTICE

Most people who stay with aikido are looking to perfect the art and have no desire to hurt anybody. What is unique to aikido is the attitude with which you train. There is no competition in the traditional form of the art, and the feeling during practice is one of mutual co-operation for the successful completion of a particular technique. The partner who applies the technique is called tori, while the one who

Above Tamura Sensei, 8th Dan Shihan, Aikikai Hombu representative to France, teaching at a seminar in Bristol, England.

Above Yamada Shihan, 8th Dan, Aikikai delegate to the USA, demonstrating sankyo at the Cardiff National Sports Centre, Wales, 1985.

receives it, uke. Uke's intention is to maintain as close a contact as is possible with tori so that the sensitivity to neutralize the effect of the movement can be developed, and in this way the situation "recovered". Training like this means that the muscles are stretched and joints are put through a wide range of natural flexion – almost like a massage. Couple this with learning how to fall safely, so that you develop the confidence to respond to the throwing techniques, and you have a complete exercise system in which strength, stamina and suppleness are simultaneously developed. All this and self-defence, too! This attitude, and the relationship between the two practitioners, means that there is no conflict, no dualism and, therefore, no violence, making it perfectly safe for men, women and children to practise.

It is true that martial arts from all over the world were originally devised to kill or to inflict injury on the battlefield. Many of these arts are extant today, even though they are no longer of any practical use, and are practised largely for reasons of cultural heritage. What tended to happen with many of the Japanese martial arts was that they underwent a socio-political change and evolved from "arts" concerned with the destruction of life into "ways" of integrating the physical and spiritual beings of practitioners to make them into better people. Thus, the art of Japanese archery kyujutsu, or "art of the bow", became kyudo, the "way of the bow". Similarly, kenjutsu, "art of the sword", became kendo, the "way of the sword", and jujutsu, "art of gentleness", became judo, the "way of gentleness". The techniques of aikijujutsu, "art of aiki", became aikido, the "way of aiki".

HOW TO USE THIS BOOK

This aikido guide is predominantly aimed at individuals with an interest in aikido who would like to make that crucial first step of joining a dojo. It gives a comprehensive overview of the subject, with individual chapters designed to promote interest without being overly involved and off-putting. Most of what constitutes traditional aikido is touched on in a way that should engender enthusiasm, while the exercises and movements are shown in a clear, simple step-by-step format.

It should be pointed out that the techniques shown in the following chapters are just a few of the hundreds that constitute aikido, and they have been picked to give an indication of the variety available in training. Virtually every defence technique has an omote (a motion to the partner's front), and a ura (a motion to the partner's back) variation, but it is beyond the scope of this book to be fully comprehensive. For clarity of understanding, some of the techniques also contain inset pictures to show the finer, sometimes unseen, aspects of the techniques.

After referring to this book it is hoped that readers will understand the extraordinary scope of aikido. We live in a world preoccupied with war, strife and technology, where the all-pervading idea reigns that to win you need to be the biggest or the fastest or the strongest. This leaves a welcome place for aikido with its philosophy of non-violence and emphasis on the spiritual. This book will have served its purpose if it inspires just one single reader to search out a qualified teacher and begin training – for that is the only way to grasp the meaning of this fascinating art.

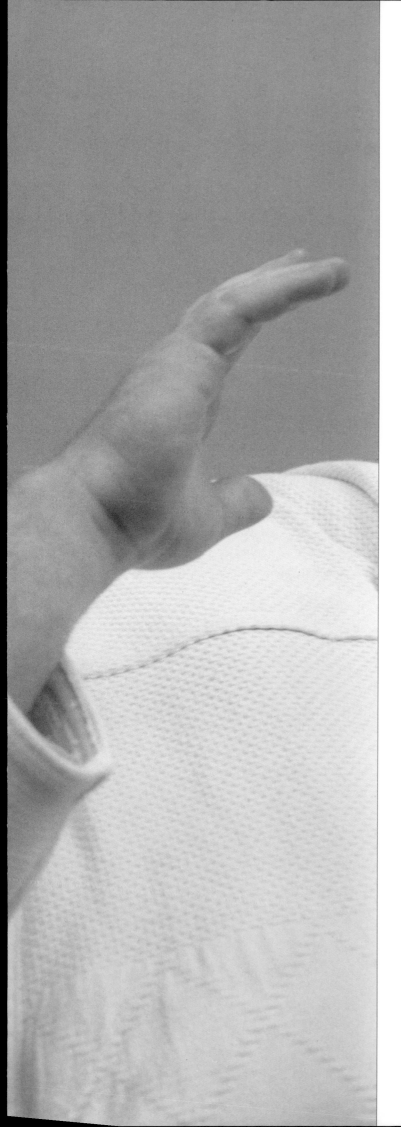

Aikido
in Context

This chapter looks at the contextual framework of aikido. The historical roots of aikido are traced through the technique of Daito ryu aiki jujutsu, which has a lineage stretching back to the 9th century. Morihei Ueshiba's role in developing the philosophical, spiritual and physical concept of aikido is covered here in detail, including the significant relationships that he had with other key figures and the strong aikido heritage that he left on his death. The traditions and etiquette integral to aikido and the way they are practised in modern dojos are also explained, along with the formal postures of the art. A section on principles and philosophy looks at centred power and the importance of mental focus and, to finish, an outline of required clothing and equipment.

Historical Background

While the name aikido came into use only in the 1940s, its origins can be traced back to the Minamoto family in 11th-century feudal Japan. Passed through the generations of this family, the principles of the art were the heritage of 19th-century Daito-ryu master Takeda Sokaku. Initially a weapons art, under Sokaku Daito ryu underwent a transformation that focused more on the grappling arts. These influences all leave their legacy in the practice of modern aikido.

The roots of aikido began about a thousand years ago with Prince Teijun, the sixth son of Japan's fifty-sixth ruler, Emperor Seiwa. He is believed to have passed on secret information concerning the principles of aiki to successive generations of the Minamoto family. Known as Seiwa Genji, the descendants of the clan kept this knowledge as their personal family art throughout the centuries. In 11th-century Japan there were two main samurai families, or clans – the Heishi and the Genji. The leader of the Genji clan was Minamoto No Yoriyoshi, who was a very powerful force on the eastern side of the country. He had two sons, one of whom was called Yoshimitsu – it is this man who is widely accepted as the founder of the tradition

Below Minamoto No Yoshimitsu (1045–1127), the son of the leader of the Genji clan, is believed to be the founder of Daito ryu aiki jujutsu.

that ultimately became Daito ryu aiki jujutsu. Yoshimitsu is reputed to have cut up the bodies of dead soldiers in an attempt to understand the bone structure of human anatomy to enable him to create more effective jujutsu techniques. Legend also has it that he once watched a spider making a web, observing that the spider could catch prey that was bigger than itself. This led him to the notion that size and strength were not so important, and that with guile it could be possible for a small person to defeat a much larger opponent.

Yoshimitsu meditated over these concepts for years and realized that the principles that made his techniques work were based on movements that occur in nature – he had discovered aiki, and in so doing had laid the foundation of Daito ryu, a tradition that still exists today. Years later, Yoshimitsu moved to a place called Kai in the Yamanashi Prefecture and took on the family name of Takeda, creating a dynasty that took control of the area until the late 16th century. The martial art started by Yoshimitsu underwent several changes and was passed on to the Aizu clan by Takeda Kunitsugu.

The Aizu was one of several warring clans and they adopted Daito ryu as their secret art, permitting only high-ranking samurai, courtiers and people of wealth to study it. The system incorporated swordsmanship, spearfighting and certain unarmed combat forms based on Aiki in-yo-ho, the doctrine of "harmony of the spirit", based on the complementary but antagonistic opposites yin and yang. The most secret of these arts was called the Oshikiuchi, taught only inside the castle to the elite warriors. The training at this time came under the authority of the head of the Shirakawa Castle and former chief councillor of the Aizu domain, Saigo Tanomo.

In 1867–8 there was civil war in Japan between the Tokugawa shogunate, or military government, and the forces of Emperor Meiji. The Aizu clan had stood with the Tokugawas, and were consequently defeated. This confrontation brought to an end more than 700 years of clan feuding and heralded the start of a ten-year period of change, the end of which saw the abolition of the wearing of two swords and, thereby, the end of samurai doctrine as it was. Many martial ryu, or schools, disbanded as there was no longer any use for the swordsmanship techniques that had been part of daily life for

Above Four men in traditional samurai costume.

Above Japanese print of a samurai warrior on the battlefield.

Above Takeda Shrine at present-day Yamanashi Prefecture.

centuries. Some staunch traditionalists went underground and trained in their arts to keep the traditions alive. It was from this environment that one person was to emerge who was to have a profound influence over the creation of aikido – Takeda Sokaku.

TAKEDA SOKAKU

It was Takeda Sokaku who resystemized Daito ryu and is credited as its founder. Born in Aizu Bangemachi in Fukushima Prefecture in 1859, the son of Takeda Sokichi, as a boy he learned kenjutsu (art of the sword), bojutsu (art of the staff) and other jujutsu forms. He was also skilled in sumo, and apparently there is to this day a sumo ring in the house where he was born as a testament to the family connection with that art. After the Meiji Restoration there was an effort to suppress the practice of martial arts in an attempt to curb any future civil insurrection. Sokaku, however, coming from a staunchly traditional samurai family, continued to practise ono-ha-itto kenjutsu under Shibuya Toma, one of the old Aizu warriors. Later, Sokaku began travelling the country searching out leading martial artists and learning all he could from them. In 1873 he became an uchideshi, or live-in student, of Sakakibara Kenkichi of the Jikishinkage ryu of kenjutsu. After the death of his older brother, Sokatsu, in 1875, Sokaku was expected to take on the role of leader in the family tradition of Shin Shoku – a Shinto tradition in which he would be expected to prepare and participate in shrine ceremonies. Sokaku, however, was not a good student – so bad was he, in fact, that he was said to be totally illiterate. Not long after this time, Sokaku resolved to forego his religious duties with the family and devote his life instead to the pursuit of martial arts.

Left Saigo Tanomo, Sokaku's mentor who made him consider the role of weapons in a society that had rejected them.

It is clear that Sokaku was the consummate martial artist, a man always on his guard and totally alert. Even on social occasions, he assumed the hanmi (back triangle stance), as can be seen in some photographs taken of him. Based mainly in Hokkaido, in the most northern part of Japan, Sokaku only occasionally visited Tokyo and the West, continuing his own austere training and teaching well into his eighties. He died in 1943 after suffering a stroke. Although Sokaku could hardly write his own name, he insisted that all students he taught record their names in his ledger (called the Eimei Roku) and considering that he is said to have taught more than 30,000 students in his lifetime, including Morihei Ueshiba, founder of aikido, this is an impressive ledger.

Below Daito-ryu master Takeda Sokaku (1859–1943) whose practice influenced the development of aikido more than any other martial art.

While there are no written records, it is said that this was the period when Sokaku was first introduced to Aiki jujutsu by Hoshina Chikanori, otherwise known as Saigo Tanomo, head of the Shirakawa Castle, who had been taught the art by Sokaku's grandfather, Soemon. Others have said that it was actually Sokichi, Sokaku's father, who taught him the arts. What is certain is that Saigo's philosophy had a profound effect on Sokaku and made him think deeply about the value of swordsmanship in a society that was beginning to evolve without practical need of it. Saigo paradoxically hired Sokaku to be his bodyguard and also to transmit to him the secret arts of the Aizu clan, known as Oshikiuchi, as he recognized within him great potential as a martial artist. Barely 1.50m (5ft) tall, Sokaku devoted his entire life to bujutsu and acquired teaching licences in okuden, or secret teachings of the ono-ha-itto-ryu (swordsmanship) and sojutsu (spearfighting) in 1877, along with Aiki jujutsu. Sokaku spent a lot of his life travelling Japan taking on anyone wishing to test his fighting skills – he was never defeated. His legendary skills gave rise to many stories – such as one where Sokaku was on a train and he became involved in a disagreement with an American teacher, Charles Parry, over the seating arrangements. Parry was a large man, but even so when tempers flared Sokaku easily restrained him using Daito ryu techniques. Impressed with this Japanese man's ability, Parry informed his superiors and word filtered through to American President Theodore Roosevelt, who requested a demonstration. A teacher was dispatched, who, after the demonstration, established a teaching regime in America. Charles Parry himself became a student and was given a teaching licence by Sokaku himself.

The Development of Aikido

Aikido founder, Morihei Ueshiba, was drawn as a young man to religious mysticism and the martial arts. He later met Takeda Sokaku, master of Daito ryu aiki jujutsu, and then Onisaburo Deguchi, leader of the Omoto-kyo movement, both of whom had a profound influence on him. Ueshiba developed his accumulated knowledge into a new art that combined his philosophical principles, immense spiritual powers and physical technique.

Aikido's founder, Morihei Ueshiba, was born on 14 December 1883 in Tanabe, present-day Wakayama Prefecture. According to his son, Kisshomaru, when Ueshiba was a small boy he saw his father being beaten up by thugs in the pay of a local politician. This experience had a profound effect on the young Ueshiba, who vowed that one day he would become strong enough to take his revenge. At the age of seven, Ueshiba's father sent him to school to study the classical Chinese texts, but he became bored with this style of education, choosing instead to engross himself in esoteric Shingon Buddhist rites and various meditative practices. Despite an interest in science and mathematics, Ueshiba felt himself increasingly drawn to religious mysticism and the martial arts. He devoted himself to hard, physical training and developed an interest in sumo to improve both his physique and his spirituality. Ueshiba started his formal education at 13 but left just a year later. He returned after a while and enrolled at the Yoshida abacus institute and, upon graduating, took a position in the Tanabe tax office, where his duties involved the assessment of land values. Much to the annoyance of his father, Ueshiba resigned his position over a local dispute about fishing legislation, and went to Tokyo to make a living in business. With his father's financial backing he established a stationery business in 1901, and it was around this time that Ueshiba began his martial arts training in jujutsu and kenjutsu. The following year, however, he contracted the vitamin-deficiency disease beriberi. As a result of this, he closed the store and moved back to Tanabe, where, on his recovery, he rekindled his relationship with Hatsu Itogawa, a childhood girlfriend, whom he subsequently married.

Above Morihei Ueshiba (1883–1969), the founder of aikido, shown in his mid-fifties when he was considered at his prime.

MILITARY SERVICE AND HOKKAIDO

In 1903 Ueshiba joined the army, where he was nicknamed "king of soldiers" due to his prowess with the bayonet, and for his dogged determination and honest character. The Russo-Japanese war broke out in 1904 and Ueshiba was sent to the front, returning as a sergeant having been promoted for bravery in the field. It was said of him that if others would do twice as much work, then he would do four

times – such was his character. During this time Ueshiba received instruction in yagyu ryu jujutsu. In 1907 his discharge from the army came through and he returned to Tanabe to take up farming, becoming involved with local politics as leader of the young men's association. At this time, his father had a dojo built on the family property and engaged the services of a high-ranking judo expert who was visiting the area to teach kodokan judo to Ueshiba. In 1910 Ueshiba embarked on an ambitious government plan to settle land in Hokkaido, an island in the north, and asked for volunteers from the young men's association. In 1912 he led a group of 54 families to start a new life in the wilderness of Shirataki. The settlers endured severe hardships during the next few years due to the hard climate and poor land, but gradually – due in no small part to Ueshiba's efforts – they began to reap rewards. And a timber business they had set up also began to return a profit.

Above A picture of Morihei Ueshiba and Onisaburo Deguchi. It was Deguchi's teachings that began to steer Ueshiba away from the pragmatic approach of Takeda towards a more spiritual dimension.

MEETING WITH TAKEDA SOKAKU

While in Hokkaido in 1915, during a stay at an inn at Engaru, Ueshiba was introduced to a man who was to change his life – Takeda Sokaku , master of Daito ryu aiki jujutsu. Immediately impressed with Sokaku, Ueshiba asked if he could become his student. He stayed at the inn for the next month and received his first teaching certificate of proficiency in Daito ryu. On his return to Shirataki, Ueshiba built a house and a dojo for Sokaku on his property and took private lessons from him every morning for many years. Historical evidence suggests that although there was a great deal of respect between them, there was no affection, and this was probably due to their differences in outlook. Sokaku was a pragmatic martial artist who had been something of a street fighter all his life, had a reputation for arrogance and was ill-tempered. Ueshiba was a deeply spiritual person whose view of martial arts was becoming channelled towards the physical and spiritual integration of the individual. Sokaku expected total loyalty and obedience from his uchideshi, or live-in students, in return for his teachings. Ueshiba gave his total dedication to Sokaku during the next four years.

MEETING WITH ONISABURO DEGUCHI

In 1919 Ueshiba received a telegram informing him that his father was gravely ill. He immediately left Hokkaido, leaving all his property to Sokaku. However, instead of travelling straight to his father's bedside in Tanabe, he stopped at Ayabe to pray for his father's recovery at the headquarters of Omoto-kyo, a new religion in Japan. Here, Ueshiba met another individual who was to influence him greatly and was to have an enormous input in the development of aikido – Onisaburo Deguchi, the charismatic leader of the Omoto-kyo movement.

The son of a student of Kotodama – the belief that the sound of certain words can result in physical manifestations – Onisaburo displayed a genius for classical study at a very early age and had a seemingly insatiable thirst for mysticism. In his lifetime he is said to have authored a massive amount of work on the subject, including one piece that numbered 81 volumes. Known as the *Reito Monogatari*, or "Tales of the Spiritual World", it concerns itself with Onisaburo's travels in the cosmos interpreting the past, present and future in terms of the Kotodama, as well as giving advice on a wide variety of mundane things, such as personal hygiene: "Men do not have an absolute right to enter the bath before women; it depends who is the dirtier." Such esoteric concepts were apparently gleaned from conversations he had with various gods and Buddhas, who had divulged their secrets to him.

Onisaburo married into the family of another mystic, a man who had developed the Omoto-kyo religious movement, and adopted their family name of Deguchi. He took over the movement and fashioned it to suit himself. He was said to have been an extremely flamboyant character, a man with a penchant for fine clothing and the company of beautiful women. With a mane of hair capped by a shaman's hat, he must have cut a dashing figure – a man who was both charismatic and irresistible as a leader.

Along with the development of the chinkon-kishin meditation techniques, Onisaburo was interested in music, composing ballads, folk songs and even dance music, including waltzes and tangos. He was also involved with calligraphy, painting and sculpture and, for a time, dabbled in directing movies. With such a wide range of interests and his charismatic qualities as a spiritual leader, it was hardly surprising that Onisaburo attracted more than just ordinary country people to his teachings. Government officials, intellectuals, aristocrats and high-ranking military men all became fascinated with this new religion, with the result that the sect expanded rapidly in popularity and became increasingly wealthy. During the period between 1919 and 1921 the cult had attracted several million devotees.

UESHIBA AND OMOTO-KYO

It is said that while Ueshiba was in meditation at the Omoto-kyo temple he had a vision of his sick father, but was advised by Onisaburo that his father was happy and that he should let him go. So under the spell of Onisaburo was Ueshiba that he stayed for a while talking with the guru and taking part in chinkon-kishin meditation sessions. When he returned to Tanabe he found that his father had indeed passed away peacefully. After a brief but intense period of misogi, or purification, involving Ueshiba going into the mountains every night and training himself like a demon swinging his bokken, or wooden sword, Ueshiba decided to move to Ayabe to avail himself more of Onisaburo's Omoto-kyo teachings. He remained there for the next eight years. Taking Onisaburo's advice, Ueshiba built a small dojo on his property to continue his martial training and to train other Omoto-kyo followers.

Early in 1921 the Omoto sect came under scrutiny by the local government, which, for political reasons, attempted to close the sect down. Onisaburo, along with several other members, was arrested. Ueshiba immersed himself in his martial training and farming, and by so doing discovered a profound connection between agriculture and the martial arts, a connection that was to remain with him for the rest of his life. After the abolition of feudalism, dating from the late 19th century, many samurai turned to farming. In this they found a spiritual connection and strong affinity between budo (literally, the "way of the combat") and working the land, as the two have traits in common, such as living honourably. Onisaburo was released on bail within two years and Ueshiba helped him rekindle interest in the Omoto-kyo religion.

SPIRITUAL ENLIGHTENMENT

Around this time Ueshiba began to move away from the pragmatic and austere qualities of the traditional martial arts and more towards spiritual ideals in his search for something to unite mind, body and spirit, as he saw this as the way forward. In 1922, after intensive study of Kotodama, he renamed his art "Ueshiba ryu aiki bujutsu". In 1924 Ueshiba and Onisaburo left for Manchuria and Mongolia to establish a "new world order" based on the ideals of Omoto-kyo. Known as The Great Mongolian Adventure, this brief period had a marked effect on Ueshiba's spiritual development. He became embroiled in several desperate situations – he was attacked with swords, shot at, arrested by a Chinese warlord and then chained and threatened with execution. He escaped death only as a result of the very fortunate intervention of the Japanese consulate. On his return to Japan Ueshiba resumed his training and farming and also began training in the art of the spear. It is said that his experiences in Mongolia had given him almost magical powers of perception, with stories of him being able to dodge a bullet. This type of intuition was to show itself many times in his later life.

Above This fine picture of Ueshiba in his later years has a serene quality, depicting a man totally at peace with himself.

Above Ueshiba in his eighties, effortlessly dispatching a young uke during a demonstration.

In 1925 Ueshiba received a visit from a naval officer, a man who was also an expert in kendo, or Japanese swordsmanship. The two of them apparently had some sort of disagreement, tempers flared and a physical encounter then ensued. The officer attacked with his bokken (wooden sword), but was unable to land a blow, as Ueshiba was able to perceive the direction of every cut before it actually happened. In the end, the officer was forced to sit down exhausted and Ueshiba went off to wash himself in a nearby well.

What happened next is an extremely well-documented experience of enlightenment for the aikido founder. While washing at the well he felt that he was bathing in a golden light pouring down from heaven. It was a revelation and he felt reborn, as if suddenly his body and spirit had been turned into gold. At the same time, the unity of the universe and the self became clear to him and he came to understand the philosophical principles on which aikido is based. It was at this time that Ueshiba changed the name of his art from aiki bujutsu to aiki budo, as aikido had now begun to transcend the boundaries of mere martial art, becoming more of a spiritual discipline. The prefix *jutsu* refers to physical technique or art, whereas *do* (pronounced *doh*) means "way" (in terms of a spiritual path).

The next few years saw Ueshiba teaching his new art to high-ranking personnel from the army and navy and the world of politics – he even spent a brief period

Above Morihei Ueshiba, founder of aikido, with Hatsu, his wife and companion for over 60 years.

teaching at the crown prince's palace in Tokyo. After deciding that his future lay in the teaching of martial arts, he obtained a property in Ushigome, in Wakamatsu-cho, in 1930 where he embarked on building a dojo. This was a massive undertaking, and during the construction phase he built a temporary dojo, and this is where Ueshiba received a visit from judo founder, Dr Jigoro Kano. Kano was so impressed with aikido, apparently declaring it as "my ideal budo", that he promptly dispatched two of his high-ranking students to train with Ueshiba. One of these was a man called Minoru Mochizuki, who remained with the founder and became one of only a handful of people ever to be awarded the rank of 10th Dan in aikido.

THE KOBUKAN DOJO

In 1931 the mighty Kobukan was built in Tokyo, on exactly the same site as the present-day facility. Consisting of an 80-mat dojo, the Kobukan attracted people from all over Japan, and in the next ten years many notable students began training there, including Shigemi Yonekawa, Rinjiro Shirata and Gozo Shioda, the latter who went on to create his own style of aikido called yoshinkan. Another student to train there was Kiyoshi Nakakura, who was to become the founder's son-in-law, but he was primarily a kendo practitioner and went on to become Japan's top exponent of the art. With the outbreak of World War II there was a dramatic effect on membership of martial dojos across the country as many of the students left the area to go off to war. The Tokyo dojo was left in the charge of Ueshiba's son, Kisshomaru.

THE MOVE TO IWAMA

Ueshiba had become physically and emotionally drained by the carnage of the war and so, with his wife, he moved to a small farm in a rural location called Iwama, which was about 130km (80 miles) or so from Tokyo. There the two of them lived a Spartan existence, but they were perfectly happy living off the land, not missing at all the frenetic activity of city life. Ueshiba had been acquiring land in the area since 1935 and now, in 1942, he owned quite a sizeable plot. He decided to build there what was to become the spiritual home of aikido – a shrine that was dedicated to the philosophy of aiki and an outdoor dojo in the Ibaraki Prefecture. And it was at about this time that Ueshiba formally changed the name of his art from aiki budo, the "aiki martial way", to the modern name of aikido, the "way of harmony".

THE SPREAD OF AIKIDO

The devastation caused during the war meant that essential services – transport, food supply and communications – were all badly affected resulting in very little activity in martial arts dojos. This, and the fact that the occupying military authorities had banned the practice of all martial arts, had closed the Tokyo dojo. The building itself was used as a shelter for people made homeless during the Allied bombing raids. In 1948 permission was given by the Japanese ministry to create an aiki foundation to promote the principles of aikido, as they were non-violent, and a year later the Tokyo dojo reopened.

Initially the dojo struggled financially, but as normality gradually returned and some of Ueshiba's pre-war students resumed their training, conditions began to flourish and new dojos were opened up all over Tokyo, including, for the first time, universities. The first public demonstration of aikido was held in 1956 and now there was interest beginning to be shown by foreign students.

A few of Ueshiba's senior students had travelled internationally and had begun to attract followers. One such senior, Abbe Kenshiro, was in Britain in the mid-1950s and is credited with being the first to show aikido in London at a judo tournament. Judo was an art in which he also excelled, along with kendo and karate. During the mid-1960s, the founder (also referred to as O'Sensei, which means "great teacher") dispatched many of his uchideshi to countries throughout the world to spread the word of aikido and establish a link with the hombu, or world headquarters, in Tokyo.

Above Budo master Abbe Kenshiro, seen here executing a judo throw, was the first to introduce aikido to Great Britain.

In the latter years of his life Ueshiba began to take things easier, immersing himself in farming and developing his own personal aikido. In addition to prayer and meditation, he became involved more with calligraphy and studying religious scriptures. He still taught aikido, mainly at the hombu and Iwama dojos, and he began to travel more – and expected his uchideshi to follow him to look after his needs. Apparently, this could be more difficult than it sounds, as Ueshiba would jump into a taxi or a train, not explaining where he was going and expecting his hapless kaban mochi, or bag carrier, to arrange tickets and expenses. Testimonies from his students reveal that acting as kaban mochi was harder than the training itself! In his final years, Ueshiba taught aikido more by example than physical demonstration, suggesting that students should make up their own mind about what they had been taught. His long lectures would be expressed in such a way that they could be interpreted at different levels. Thus Ueshiba would encourage the students to think for themselves and not to be continually led.

As founder of aikido, Ueshiba received many awards from various organizations in Japan and from abroad – he was even recognized by the emperor in 1964. But on 26 April 1969 Morihei Ueshiba died at the age of 86. On his deathbed he is supposed to have said that aikido was for the whole world and that he himself had only scratched the surface.

Above The founder executing the ikkyo arm pin in suwariwaza, or kneeling technique.

Traditions and Etiquette

To understand the culture of aikido, students must have sympathy with the ritualized traditions that were practised in feudal Japan. This is why, in so many ways, aikido is unique in its outlook compared with other martial arts that use more direct fighting skills. The strict rules of behaviour and comportment in aikido also help to reduce the practitioner's sense of ego, a state of mind that should be at the core of any serious aikido student.

A NON-AGGRESSIVE APPROACH

It is not uncommon to associate martial arts with the idea of using greater skill, speed, strength and aggression to subdue an attacker – understandable considering how many martial arts such as karate, judo, kendo and kung fu, to mention a few, encourage this outlook. There is nothing wrong with healthy competition as a measure of the success of one's personal training compared with another's. However, problems arise when the obsession to win becomes greater than the winning itself. Unfortunately, this can be a consequence of competitive training and, if the martial artist is not aware, can result in the overdevelopment of the ego with its "win at all costs" regime.

THE RATIONALE OF AIKIDO

Most martial arts deal with conflict in terms of the physical encounter, exponents using their skills to overcome a situation once it has begun. Where aikido differs dramatically is in its ethic of not dealing with conflict. Aikido does not seek to engage in conflict at all, preferring to stifle an aggressive intent long before it develops into physical confrontation.

Below Principal and founder of the UKA, Shihan W. J. Smith executing kokyu-nage against a punch, UKA Summer School, 2004.

The aikidoka (a person who practises aikido) believes that the highest level of martial art is when an aggressor is defeated without that person realizing it has happened.

The aim of the aikidoka is to diffuse an encounter in such a way that a potential foe is transformed into a potential ally, without ever surrendering or capitulating in any way. Of course, it may not always happen this way and confrontation may become inevitable – in which case the aikidoka is armed with technique. To the exponent of aikido, the physical encounter is a much lower-level use of aikido strategy, and is consequently only ever used when all else has failed.

Aikido believes that weakness is not an answer to conflict, and neither is excessive brutality. Consequently the techniques themselves are applied with an attitude of controlling an attacker without causing undue harm. This ethic can be confusing for the casual observer. On the one hand, aikido is a martial art, or is it? Some noted texts on aikido suggest that it isn't a martial art in the generally accepted sense because it does not condone conflict and does not talk of cutting down an enemy. If you move harmoniously with an attacker, then you are not entering into a conflict. Similarly, if one neutralizes an enemy, then why is it necessary to destroy him? If you make a friend out of an enemy, how is this just martial art?

CONTROL WITHOUT DAMAGE

Aikido is more than a martial art, it is a martial "way" (or *do* in Japanese, indicating an art that has transcended just physical technique, incorporating various spiritual and philosophical ideals) and embodies the highest levels of ethics in martial training. It centres on controlling and neutralizing one's opponent. This focus distinguishes aikido from competitive arts that teach exponents to punch or kick another competitor. Aikido teaches that conflict is to be avoided – this in itself is extremely rare in martial arts. The ideal is that an opponent is controlled without necessarily causing injury. Many of the techniques were modified by the founder at different stages of the art's development. In later years, as he became more spiritual, he took away some of the more dangerous elements of technique so that they could embody his vision of harmony and peace. Very few techniques involve direct pressure against the same way regardless – this also applies to weapon training. Chiba Sensei, a Japanese aikido teacher and an internationally acknowledged master of aiki weapons, once said during a seminar that: "If you know how to do shomen-uchi [a frontal cut with a sword or empty hand], then you can do aikido." And the truth is that so much that is done in aikido depends on understanding this relatively simple action.

The effectiveness of aikido develops from controlling the course of an attack from when it is perceived, preferably before it is launched, then blending with it, rather than blocking it, and coming back with a countermove. One harmonizes with the attack and leads it to a point of exhaustion before applying a technique of neutralization. This is one of the cornerstones of aikido practice, the principle permeating every aspect of aikido strategy.

THE SWORD OF THE SAMURAI

In feudal Japan when a samurai visited another's house, he would surrender his long sword and retain his short sword. If you entered someone's house and their wall-mounted sword was hung with its tip facing the door, you had to be careful because this person did not trust anyone. A sword mounted with its handle facing the door meant that its owner trusted the people admitted. This same etiquette is observed today in dojos that display a katana kake, or sword rack. If a samurai allowed the saya, or scabbard, of his sword to knock the saya of another samurai, it was considered a gross insult that could be resolved only by the drawn sword and the spilling of blood. To be invited to inspect another samurai's sword at his home was considered an honour. But if you got it wrong, it was considered an insult.

Typically, you were offered the sword held in its owner's left hand in its scabbard with the cutting edge facing him. The sword held in the owner's right hand with the cutting edge towards the recipient was considered an offensive act.

Above Future masters learning their craft – two young enthusiasts practise aikido at a children's class in Birmingham, England.

the natural movement of the joints. The idea is that the joints are stretched in a natural direction a little farther than they could go on their own. Consequently, after a practice your body feels revitalized as opposed to uncomfortable.

A PRACTICE FOR ALL

Although aikido can be practised by men, women and children, research has shown that repetitive stretching of young joints can result in problems in later life. So in Great Britain, for example, certain joint techniques are eliminated from children's practice. The founder taught that one should move so as to close off all openings for attack when engaging an opponent and he structured the techniques to incorporate this ideal. This meant that all techniques, whether basic, intermediate or advanced would be the same in terms of body movement. This, coupled with the concept of musubi, or "tying together", laid the foundation for a defence system that is comprehensive in the way it deals with an attack. In the mind of the aikidoka, all techniques are one, as the body moves in

Below The katana kake, or sword rack, is used to exhibit the katana (long sword) and the saya (scabbard).

Above Tamura Sensei demonstrating a move in front of his attentive students.

The recipient would accept the sword as it was given him, by the left hand, turning the cutting edge towards him quickly. The person inspecting the sword would by now have placed a special cloth in his mouth to absorb the moisture in his breath – lest it go onto the blade. Allowing the breath to reach the blade would almost certainly have transmitted damp and bacteria and so begun the process of rusting – and would not have been taken lightly. The inspector of the sword would then slowly draw the blade from its scabbard with his left hand and, with a piece of washi, a type of paper cloth, wipe away any oil or deposits from the bottom to the top of the blade. Then he would apply some uchiko powder to absorb any moisture on the blade and wipe from bottom to top. After completing his inspection he would wipe the blade again and apply a light coating of oil before slowly returning the sword to its scabbard and returning it to the owner, as described above. The slightest deviation from this etiquette would not be tolerated.

OBSERVING ETIQUETTE

The etiquette used in traditional aikido dojos is a distillation of that used in feudal Japan – the difference being that in feudal times, non-observance of certain etiquette could result in a fight to the death. While contemporary aikidokas may not be under that pressure, disregarding dojo etiquette contributes to a watering down of tradition and an erosion in the transmission of the art. When we disregard etiquette we lose

some of the oriental quality of aikido, and what it is that separates what we do in the dojo from what goes on in exercise rooms elsewhere. Etiquette is discipline and respect, and a dojo without these qualities is a dangerous place to be, particularly when weapons are involved. Japan's infrastructure was based very much on the sempai/kohai (senior/junior) relationship, a strict hierarchical system. Originally, the samurai (whose name means "one who serves") would be employed by a daimyo, a feudal lord, to fulfil their every demand. If he ever brought his lord into disrepute or grossly failed in a task, he would ask for permission to commit suicide (formally – seppuku) or ritual suicide, which entailed him disembowelling himself with a knife seconds before a helper (the kaishaku) beheaded him with a sword to end his agony.

BASIC DOJO ETIQUETTE

It is difficult for the Western mind to comprehend this behaviour, yet in those days it was considered honourable. Yet we see many examples of indigenous customs that we may find strange. We accept these as being "different" from our own and acknowledge that traditions are a trait that distinguishes one culture from another. If we disregard these traditions we lose sight of what that race is and how it has evolved. In traditional aikido dojos the etiquette is stringent when compared with other martial arts, and aikido has retained its Japanese quality all the more for it. If you join a club that is affiliated to the International Aikido Federation (IAF), it does not matter if you live in Europe, Asia, North or South America, the etiquette is the same. Here are some examples:

- When entering a dojo, a tachi rei (standing bow) is performed in the direction of the kamiza, meaning "seat of the gods", an area usually in the centre of the wall opposite the entrance. There may be a wooden structure to house a picture of aikido's founder and perhaps a scroll containing calligraphy of the Japanese kanji for "aikido". There may also be a katana kake (sword rack) and wooden weapons. Sometimes flowers are displayed, or simply a picture of the founder.

- The class lines up, kneeling, with the sensei (teacher) at the front and the students in front of the shimoza (opposite wall), with the sempai (senior students) to the right of the dojo facing the kamiza. The instructor uses the command Hai, which means "Yes". (At some dojos, "shomen ni rei" is said, which means "bow to the front".) The whole class responds by bowing while saying "onegaishimasu", which means "please teach me". The sensei then faces the members of the class, who then all bow to him or her. At some dojos the sempai say "sensei ni rei", which means "bow to sensei".

- If you are late for a class, you must wait at the side of the tatami (mat) until given permission to join the class by the sensei. You then perform a seiza (formal kneeling) bow in the direction of the kamiza.

- Engage in some warm-up exercises and then join the class by saying to a fellow practitioner "onegaishimasu", meaning "please teach me".

- The sensei indicates the end of the class with a hand clap, when everyone lines up as before. The etiquette is the same as at the start, but the utterance is now "domo arigato gozaimashita" ("thank you very much"). A lower-ranked student will generally fold the sensei's hakama (pleated, pants) after practice, and this is considered an honour.

During practice, talking is kept to a minimum with full focus on what is being said and taught by the sensei. Aikido is taught mainly by demonstration, with students copying what they see to the best of their ability and repeating it over and over.

   A bokken (wooden sword) is treated as a live blade, as is the jo (a staff). The bokken was a practice weapon for the samurai, who used it rather than a real sword to avoid the lethal cutting power of a live blade. It can still cause damage, however, and has to be respected. When making the salutation at the start of the class, the handle of the bokken is held in the left hand, cutting edge toward you, with the right hand underneath holding the blade near the tip. A standing bow toward the kamiza is then made. The students make the same bow to the sensei. At the end of the class, the same thing happens in reverse – everyone bows first to the sensei and then to the kamiza. You do not touch someone else's bokken without invitation. When the weapon is at its owner's side, it is bad manners to step over it and you should not touch its cutting edge.

Above Students sitting in seiza as they watch their instructor demonstrating.

Below left and right Two practitioners face each other, before bowing in seiza rei. This is the bow of a student to their teacher or of two students showing respect to each other prior to, or after training.

Seiza (Formal Kneeling)

These front, side and rear views show the formal kneeling posture known as seiza.
There should be a feeling of stability as you mentally perceive the two knees and the feet
behind as a triangle – the most stable form in nature.

Hold the hands either in a loosely closed fist or with the fingers straight, pointing slightly inwards and resting on the thighs. The knees should be about two to three fist-widths apart.

Keep the spine straight and the chin tucked in.

The big toes can either touch, as here, or be crossed.

Seiza Rei (Formal Kneeling Bow)

This sequence shows the correct way to execute a formal bow from the kneeling position.

1 Start off in the seiza position, shown above.

2 Place the left hand on the tatami.

3 Place the right hand on the tatami, fingers angled in towards each other. You have formed a triangle with your elbows, hands and forearms placed so that should an enemy try to push your head to the floor your hands would cushion the impact.

4 As you lean forward to bow, remember never to show the nape of your neck to your opponent – it was considered bad manners, not to mention dangerous, to lose sight of him. Reverse these steps to return to the start position.

Tachi Rei (Formal Standing Bow)

This is the formal standing bow that is used as an everyday standard in Japanese society. The tachi rei is a polite, courteous greeting and has more or less the same meaning as shaking hands in western culture.

1 Begin by standing straight with the palms of both hands resting on the front of the thighs and fingers pointing slightly inwards. Your eyes should be looking forward, directed at the object, or person, to which you are bowing.

2 Bending from the waist, keep the upper body straight and bow forward. Lower your eyes as you make the bow and then return them to looking forward at the object of your bow as you straighten again to the start position.

The kamiza (seat of the gods)

This is the focal point of the dojo, usually consisting of a wooden structure styled with a Japanese feel. It traditionally houses a picture of aikido's founder, Morihei Ueshiba. A scroll with the kanji of aikido can also be hung in this area. Weapon racks containing bukken (long wooden swords) or jo (short swords) are also common, as are flower arrangements. The whole class faces the kamiza when the session begins and at the command "hai" everyone bows to O'Sensei's picture. The attitude is of thanking the founder's spirit for showing the way to enlightenment.

Principles and Philosophy

There are a number of key principles to absorb as a new student of aikido. The idea of centred power, enabling coordination of mind and body, is a core concept, along with the importance of using circular, spherical and spiral moves rather than blocks, and the emphasis of non-resistance over technique. Finally, there is the inspiration drawn from the harmonies evident within the natural world, and the influence of the principles of yin and yang.

CENTRALIZATION

When you begin aikido training you will be guided through a system of exercises – physical and mental – designed to make you "think from your belly", meaning the centre of gravity of the human body, which lies bout 5cm (2in) below the navel and a little way inward (depending how big your belly is).This central point, known variously as the tanden, hara or seika no itten, is considered in the Far East not just as the physical centre of the body, but also its spiritual centre.

Below The seiza, or formal kneeling posture gives a feeling of stability from the balanced, triangular position of the knees and feet.

Awareness of the tanden is the first leg of the journey to becoming a physically and spiritually integrated human, and the goal of your training is the total coordination of the mind and body. Imagine a central axis from the top of your head down through your body and out through the floor, with the point of emphasis being the tanden – it is with such awareness that all movements in aikido are made. This idea of the "centre" is then expanded to include one's relationship with the environment and, ultimately, the universe. It is not only the Japanese martial arts that have awareness of the centre as a prerequisite, but also Chinese, Russian and Indian arts. Indian yoga teaches us of the "serpent power of the Kundalini", which equates to the same thing.

CENTRED POWER

The power that can be generated by a person who is centred can be extraordinary, with adepts being able to resist being lifted, pushed over or moved in any way. The founder of aikido can be seen famously on film sitting down cross-legged, resisting the attempts of several students simultaneously pushing on his forehead to unseat him. They all end up on the floor with a shake of his head.

Having developed awareness of your centre, the next step is to maintain that awareness while executing techniques with a partner. Sitting silently meditating in a room is a far cry from dealing with several attackers – this is the real test of your ability to reach into the power of the centre.

EXTENSION

Having found your centre you then have to learn how to extend power from it. The traditional way is to experience this within the framework of the techniques. If a technique fails, it is usually down to a lack of centredness and, thus, no extension of energy. A Japanese sensei would probably say that a student has "no kokyu", or no breath power, if this happens – breath power being the vehicle that transmits ki, or spirit energy, from the centre.

Aikido holds that this energy can be harnessed in the centre of gravity and then channelled through the body to the fingertips into technique. Aikidokas aim to keep this extension

Above The bokken cut is made up and down the centre line of the body. The blade is projected above the target and cuts along the backstroke.

Above The final cut of irimi-nage where tori is about to take uke down by rotating his arm and sticking his thumb into the floor.

turned on at all times so that they are always generating power. This extension of energy can be likened to the emanation of water from the ground that runs into a spring that feeds into a river. As long as the water exudes continuously from its source no impurities from the river can get to that source. So, if you extend your mind forcefully your arms will not bend and they will become like a shield against attack.

Many practitioners of traditional aikido like to practise the weapon work associated with it: the bokken (a wooden sword), the jo (a 1.2m/4ft long oak staff that replaces the traditional spear) and the tanto (a wooden or rubber knife that replaces a real blade). These weapons complement perfectly the idea of extension from the centre, particularly the bokken and jo, which require both hands to hold the weapon. In this way, the hands are automatically held in line with the centre line of the body, making it easier to imagine extension from your centre and up through the weapon towards your partner.

If your partner grabs your right wrist and you assume the hanmi posture (see step 1 on page 54), and extend that arm in line with your central axis in a particular direction, as long as you concentrate forcefully on the idea of energy coming up through the floor, through your centre to your fingertips, your partner will be sent hurtling away with a surprising force. The ultimate use of extension is within a multiple attack, where you are at the centre of the action whirling in their midst like a tornado, repelling the aggressors in the same way.

CIRCULAR, SPHERICAL AND SPIRAL MOTION

There are few examples of straight-line movement in aikido. Even when we move directly forward it is with a slightly circular body motion. The reason for this is that the basic strategy for dealing with a straight-line attack, such as an overhead strike

to the front of the head or a direct punch to the face, is to move in a circular fashion off that line. When the attack itself is more circular, as an attack to the side of the head or face, then the evasive movement is either to move off the centre line and overwhelm the attack before it has generated any power (if the attack has launched), or step inside it with a circular motion to neutralize it (if the attack is well into motion).

There are no blocks in aikido, only parries and deflections. Blocking goes against the flow of energy and may not work if the attacking force is too great. With aikido strategy, it does not matter how much attacking force is used, as you are not there to receive it. If we take the example of shomen-uchi irimi-nage ura (the front-head strike shown on page 75), the initial movement is to parry the attack and step circularly around it to a position whereby you are right behind and close to your attacker, effectively with your attacker's back on your chest and both of you looking in the same direction. From here it is easy to lead his energy in a large circle destroying his balance (kuzushi). As his weight falls, you add your own body weight to the motion and send him spinning around your centre. At the point where he tries to regain his balance, you switch your body weight from one foot to the other, causing him to lose his balance the other way. It only remains to step in and cut across his neck and face to effect a throw.

These circular, spherical or spiral movements are irresistible. If we draw on our experience of the natural world, the spiral is seen as a most powerful force. If we look at phenomena such as tornados, hurricanes and whirlpools and, further afield, at black holes and galaxies – they are all examples of forces generated by, or containing, circular and spiral motion. At the other end of the scale, all molecular activity is circular with atoms spinning around a nucleus.

Right This tranquil scene shows the sky (yin), the land (yang) and water. When agitated by lunar movements and the weather, the water can produce great force (yang), but otherwise is calm (yin).

When confronted with gyaku hanmi katate-dori (a wrist grab), for example, at the instant you are gripped you make a tenkan (turning movement), leading your attacker's energy by extending your energy from your centre and joining with that of your attacker's. You move with the idea that you are centred and that the central axis of your movement is a straight line from your head through to the floor. Next, your own body becomes the overall centre of the entire motion with your attacker spinning out of control on the periphery.

Instead of prioritizing strength, speed and force, aikido emphasizes non-resistance, saying "when pulled, enter; when pushed, turn". Every technique, body movement and cutting motion with the arms operates in circles and spirals. Standing alone with their arms extended, aikidokas extend their consciousness all around themselves in a protective sphere, and any attacker entering that sphere will be repelled.

PHILOSOPHY OF AIKIDO

Phrases used to describe the basic doctrine of aikido include "To practise aikido is to learn how to harmonize with nature" or "Aikido is the budo of love." They all encompass the real spirit of aikido. Problems can arise in interpretation, however. Many people ask themselves how a martial art can be related to love, or how the subjugation of another individual can be in harmony with nature? It is only by interpreting the words correctly that the answers reveal themselves. If we look at the land, sky, seas, trees, grass and listen to the winds and feel the heat of the sun, we see that this is nature in all its glory. But how do we reconcile this to aikido?

Right The rotary movement called kaiten (see page 50) exemplifies the concept of yin and yang. When faced with a strong attack the idea is to parry, not block, the force. By turning off the line of the attack and letting it carry on, the parry harmonizes with it.

YIN AND YANG

For thousands of years in the East there has been the belief that all phenomena are governed by antagonistic but complementary opposites, known as "yin and yang" in China, "in and yo" in Japan and "tamasic and rajasic" in India. The yin-yang symbol shows a circle divided by two shapes of identical size – one black, one white. We also see a small circle of black in the white part and of white in the black. The outer circle represents "the whole" – call it god or nature or whatever – while the black and white "fish" shapes represent the two opposites of the whole that interact and cause it to exist. The symbolism denoted in the small, opposite-coloured circles in each segment states that nothing in nature is *completely* opposite, and contains elements of its opposite.

This concept is borne out on every level of existence. The white shape within the circle is known as yin, and associated characteristics are: expansive, upward, lightness, cold and fast. The black shape is yang and is characterized by contraction, downward, heaviness, heat and slow. When you think about this you realize that virtually every natural phenomena can be explained in terms of yin and yang.

MUTUALLY DEPENDENT FORCES

Many forces of nature exist in a state of flux, opposite yet mutually dependent, drawn to each other yet repelled. Some are obvious, while others require more thought when applying the yin-yang principle. Think of the relationship of man and woman. As a general classification, women are yin with characteristics such as: feminine, gentle, soft, receptive, quiet, hairless and passive. Men are generally yang, with the following traits: masculine, violent, hard, aggressive and loud. But these are crude categorizations; what makes the whole thing so fascinating is that in reality men and women exhibit qualities of yin and yang in varying degrees. It is perfectly normal to have men with many of the attributes of yin and women with varying degrees of yang attributes. When you consider the yin-yang symbol, this notion falls in line with the thinking behind the two small circles in their respective halves – nothing is completely yin or completely yang, merely varying degrees of both.

Ki and Kokyu

Ki is a profound concept, one not easily grasped, and has stretched the abilities of undoubtedly intelligent and lucid people. It is the force that gives life to every living thing; the essence that makes us breathe, that makes our blood flow; that maintains all molecular activity. The word kokyu refers to breath power in terms of respiration. It is the process of breathing, but it can also be interpreted as the respiration of the universe and the flow of the opposing forces of nature.

The word aikido loosely means "way of harmonizing the spirit". Ai is "harmony"; ki is "spirit"; and do is "way". In a much grander sense, it is the power that energizes nature and the universe itself. Ueshiba's message through aikido was to harmonize one's own ki with the ki of the universe. He felt this was the way for humanity to reconcile itself and become one with nature and, thus, make the world a better place in which to live. To do this, we have to try to understand what ki is within the individual, how to experience it and how to channel its force.

USING KI IN YOUR DAILY LIFE

The person who can explain ki and how to develop it in an A+B+C=D manner has not been born yet and anyone who makes that claim is to be treated with suspicion. There are, however, a few mental and physical exercises you can do to promote its development. If you look at people who are experts in any field, you will see that they make what they do look easy. Take an electrician, for instance; he could be

Left The instinctive power generated by an infant's grip can be intense, and an excellent example of the power of the unconscious coordination of mind and body, or ki.

engaged with you in conversation while he is putting the wires into a plug and the part of the brain looking after the plug is on autopilot and so he is effortlessly able to complete this task and talk, too. This is an example of mind and body coordination. When you begin something new you have to work hard learning all the steps necessary to complete the process. Then you need to repeat it again and again until it becomes second nature. Only then will the skills you have acquired come out naturally. This is the natural learning process, and is particularly apt when talking about martial arts as repetition is vital to ultimate success.

RELEASING THE POWER OF KI

The power we are talking about can show itself in different and dynamic ways, such as in situations of stress. One woman in America managed to lift a truck off her small son and so save his life after he had become trapped. She cracked several vertebrae in the process, but it shows the power that is within the human body. There have been many documented cases of people tearing doors off their hinges to save people trapped inside burning buildings, and then ignoring the pain of severe burns to perform their acts of heroism. Where does this power come from? Very young children are also capable of generating enormous power – if you have ever held out a finger and let an infant grab hold of it you will know how true this can be.

These are examples of ki – a power that can be tapped only with unconscious coordination of mind and body. If you try to rationalize or intellectualize in a stressful situation, the force will not emerge. It has to be instinctive, with no gap between perception and reaction. So, a young infant has no information to draw on, its mind is a clean slate and any actions it takes are instinctive. When the child grabs your finger it probably is not even aware of doing it as it gazes around not looking at anything particularly, but taking in everything in general.

The conclusion from this must be that everyone has an extraordinary power inside that may only surface naturally in extreme circumstances. Alternatively an expert or master in any field can exhibit ki as a result of not having to think

consciously about what they are doing, in other words when mind and body are as one. So when you hear of a karate master breaking two house bricks with one blow, or an aikido exponent resisting the attempts of several people to move him, know that you are witnessing the power of ki.

DEVELOPMENT OF KI

Aikidokas attempt to harness the power of ki and to use it at will. This is not an easy endeavour, but one that must be undertaken if progress is to be made. It is too simplistic to assume that if you practise diligently, ki will emerge automatically. You have to cultivate the right mental attitude for that to happen. One of the biggest problems you will encounter in the quest for ki is bringing the wandering mind to rest. Some people can do this more easily than others. Before you can contemplate ki you need to be able to focus your mind. If you feel that you need it, there are ways you can learn to concentrate more effectively. Zazen (seated meditation) is one way; the ancient Indian system of yoga is another.

CONCENTRATION AND IMAGINATION

During the breathing process described opposite, you must imagine that the exhalation represents an expansion feeling from your centre of gravity, coupled with the notion that all the impurities of the day are being expelled with the breath. When any thoughts come, try to deftly turn them away, but not with any sort of forceful effort, as this will disturb a focused mind. In time you will be able to reach a calm and serene state of mind and, effectively, think of nothing. Of course, during the act of breathing, breath only goes in and out of your lungs. The route it

takes in the exercise is purely imaginary, but this awareness is essential to achieving the desired results. While zazen is not practised to achieve anything other than zazen, it does develop single-minded concentration and a sense of understanding of where the tanden, or your centre of gravity is.

This is a major part of Zen Buddhism, where exponents can sit looking at a plain wall for hours at a time. You may think this seems a waste of time, but in reality it is time very well spent as the degree of single-minded concentration that can be achieved is awesome. One of the difficulties in any martial art is maintaining a calm, clear mind in the midst of a frenzied onslaught from multiple attackers. If you are able to switch your consciousness in any direction instantaneously, and with total commitment, you will be coordinated and able to liberate ki energy. We have to develop a strong centre and be able to extend power from that place. Some Japanese masters recommend zazen meditation, although it is by no means essential. You may have good powers of concentration naturally, in which case it is not necessary. And there are large, very successful aikido organizations that do not include zazen in their curriculum. However, as an individual you need to develop single-mindedness to the extent that you are not readily distracted, particularly in stressful situations, and zazen practice is an excellent discipline to help you achieve this goal.

Once Chiba Sensei, the first official UK representative from the Aikido World Headquarters in Japan, was asked what ki is. His reply was that ki is the physical

Right This exercise for developing kokyu involves two people holding the other. Tori needs to harmonize with and deflect their power, otherwise he will be overcome.

manifestation of the power of the imagination. The more positive the mind, the greater the degree of imagination and, therefore, the ki that is generated is more powerful. The mind can be exercised like the body, and the more it is exercised the stronger it will become.

KOKYU (BREATH)

In the physical sense, kokyu is understood as the process of breathing which, of course, is inhalation and exhalation. In another sense, as mentioned earlier, it can be interpreted as the respiration of the universe, the natural flow of the opposing forces of nature, positive and negative. You may view the flow of day into night and the tides of the sea coming in and going out as perennial examples of kokyu. To employ kokyu successfully within aikido you must learn to harmonize your body with that of an attacker, in the same way that the forces of nature harmonize with each other, for only then is the whole achieved. These forces do not collide with one another; instead they work together to achieve harmony. A mighty oak tree that has stood for hundreds of years can be uprooted when hit with the force of a whirlwind, yet a blade of grass at the tree's base will toss and turn in the direction of the wind and consequently not be destroyed. In this sense, the grass is stronger than the tree. If we can think like this when practising aikido, what kind of power do we possess?

CULTIVATING KOKYU RYOKU (BREATH POWER)

To understand kokyu, you need to develop an awareness of the tanden, your centre of gravity, also referred to as "the one point". Zazen (seated meditation) is good for this, as are the following exercises. There are also specific exercises within the framework of aikido to help you understand the concept of kokyu. Called kokyu-ho, or breathing method, they enable you to generate the power used in all aikido techniques.

Breathing and zazen

First, find somewhere that is warm and comfortable where you will not be disturbed – preferably a matted area. Traditionalists use a zafu, which is a small round cushion, placed under the buttocks, though you should sit only on the edge of the cushion rather than square on, so that your knees can drop down towards the ground. The posture of either the full or half lotus can be used, but equally good is the seiza posture (pictured right), although this can be hard on the knee joints initially. Whatever method you use, make sure that you mentally perceive a straight line from the top of your head, through your chin to your centre of gravity. Half close your eyes and fix your gaze on the floor about 1.5m (5ft) in front of you. Close your mouth and place your

tongue on the upper palate. Try to clear your mind and think of nothing, which is not as easy as you might think. Relax all your muscles, starting from the feet upwards. When you reach the head, sit

and simply be aware of your posture and breathing – long breaths, in through the nose, and long breaths, out from the mouth. Do not sniff as you inhale, but control the inhalations with the epiglottis at the back of the throat. Enter totally the world of breathing and direct the breath through the nose and (in your mind's eye) up to the top of your head. The breath travels down your spine to its midpoint, then across to the tanden, a point about 5cm (2in) below the navel and the same distance inward (this equates to a person's centre of gravity). At the tanden, imagine that your breath is coiling up, just as if it were a spring – a contracting and, at the same time, a cleansing process. Exhalation is the reverse: your breath goes back the way it came, but instead of being expelled through the nose, you use your mouth.

Suwariwaza Kokyu-ho

The most basic of the exercises for developing breath power is called suwariwaza, or seated kokyu-ho. Remember, this exercise is not a test of strength, but an extension of the power from the tanden.

1 The uke (the practitioner who receives the technique) is holding both wrists of the tori (the practitioner who applies the technique). In the basic form, the wrists are held at chudan (middle) height. There are several variations.

2 Tori leans his body weight forward and raises his arms, as if cutting up with two swords, causing uke's elbows to be raised and destroying his power. This takes away uke's capacity to generate any strength.

3 Finally by cutting over uke's left hand with his right and spiralling his left handblade toward uke's armpit, tori is able to displace uke's centre of gravity and cause him to fall. Uke rolls naturally to the side.

4 Tori extends from his centre imagining that he is holding down the centre of the earth, and disregarding uke's hold. Uke offers token resistance to test tori's stability.

Tachiwaza Kokyu-ho

The next stage is to practise the standing form of the same exercise, which is called tachiwaza, or standing kokyu-ho. These are the basic forms of kokyu-ho practice, but it can be practised from a variety of attacks.

1 Uke holds tori's right wrist with both his hands.

2 Tori steps to the side of uke, aligning his body, and begins to cut upwards as if raising a sword in the centre line of his body. This enables tori to lift up his arms using his centre of gravity.

3 Tori now steps behind uke and by extending his arm across uke's body destroys her balance. By turning his hips and leaning his bodyweight forward, tori causes uke to fall.

THE TANDEN AND THE CENTRE LINE OF THE BODY

It quickly becomes clear from practising these kokyu methods that the power supplied for every technique comes from the tanden, which is on the centre line of the body in the lower abdomen. From this it follows that in order to move someone you have to displace that person's centre of gravity with your own. In the case of the sitting kokyu-ho, your posture, when kneeling, automatically assumes a triangle composed of your two spread knees and the feet behind.

From the stability of the triangle (the most stable form in nature) we generate power through the tanden and extend it through the arms to the fingertips, as if projecting a high-pressure stream of water from the centre of gravity. As we lean our gravity forward with these ideas in mind, we generate an incredible force on our partner as he tries to maintain a grip on the wrists. The net result is that he is moved without any recourse to muscular power from the arms or shoulders.

The same applies to the basic standing technique. Here we lean our centre of gravity into our partner's grip from an initial triangular posture, turn to the side, deflecting her force, and then, by cutting up the centre line of the body from the centre and aligning the feet by her side, you create too much force for her to maintain her grip and posture. It only remains to continue cutting upwards and over her neck in a spiral motion to cause her to lose her balance.

RELAXATION AND ALIGNMENT

No matter how you are attacked, it is crucial to harmonize with that attack and then align your body in such a way that you can use your centre of gravity, your tanden, to generate the power necessary to effect a technique. Only in this way can a smaller, weaker person overcome a larger, stronger opponent. This is a practical application of kokyu and one reason why so many women are attracted to aikido, as women, in the main, do not have the physical strength to cope with a male aggressor.

Extending power from the tanden only ever works when the body is relaxed. Putting muscular tension into these movements only serves to shut the power off – much as would happen if you kinked a hose while water was surging through it. The kokyu-ho movements are natural in that they promote the idea of deflecting your opponent's power, not receiving it. It follows, therefore, that you must practise in a relaxed manner and not try to force your partner down, otherwise your partner will sense this and fight against your technique. When you drink a glass of wine, you don't grip the glass with enough force to break it. Similarly, when you

Above In hidari hanmi, or left posture, the hands are held in the centre line of the body. The body itself is angled at 45 degrees to the front. From this position rapid front and rear movement is possible.

hold the steering wheel of a car, you don't grip it so strongly that you lose manoeuvrability. If you stand and tense your body you may feel strong and stable, but in reality you are weak and can be very easily moved. In aikido, the more relaxed you are, the more stable you are and, consequently, the more power you can generate. It is vital, however, to be centred by being aware of your tanden and that every movement (in your mind's eye) originates from there. Through repetitive practice you will come to realize that if you have the centre behind every movement you make, then you maximize your body's potential to generate power.

In summary, when we stand in the triangular posture of aikido, with hands extended on the centre line of the body, we are in the most stable form possible. We learn to concentrate our mind in our tanden through a variety of means: meditation, breathing exercises, torifune and furitama (see pages 40 and 41) and the kokyu-ho exercises themselves. We can then move on to the next stage, which is to extend power out from our newly discovered centre. If we imagine with full commitment that power is extending from the tanden out of the fingertips then it will really happen.

Clothing and Equipment

It was Jigoro Kano, the judo founder, who first initiated the design of a long-sleeved, long-trousered suit for practitioners, later adopted by aikido professionals. The long sleeves and trousers he devised were to replace earlier suits where the sleeves came above the elbows and the trousers above the knees, a design that caused many scrapes and cuts during practice. The hakama, worn only by senior grades, was originally used to protect clothing and the samurai's legs from painful friction when on horseback.

KEIKOGI

The standard practice suit, or keikogi, used for aikido is generally the same as that used in judo. The wrap-over jacket has to be able to withstand the rigours of being gripped at the collar, shoulder and sleeve during training and is consequently made of a thicker, more robust cotton than, for example, the karate-style suit, where gripping is limited. The trousers again are usually reinforced at the knees and are tied around the waist by a drawstring fed through the waistband. The suit comes complete with a white obi (belt) made of thick cotton. When you buy a keikogi, it is best to purchase one at least a size bigger than for normal clothing, as it can shrink dramatically on its first washing.

HAKAMA

The hakama, or divided skirt, is traditionally worn on formal occasions only by the upper classes of Japanese society. In aikido, it is worn only by yudansha, or dan grades, although permission to wear it is sometimes given to a person who has provided an outstanding service to a club or organization, and women can be given special dispensation, too. The hakama can be made of cotton or a mixture of cotton and polyester or Rayon, and it is available in heavy or lightweight grades. The traditional colours are black or blue. With some you must be careful that the dye does not transfer to the keikogi during a hot practice session. At the end of a training session it is traditional to fold the hakama on the tatami (practice mat) to preserve its shape, and this takes quite a while to do properly. It is considered an honour to fold the sensei's hakama after a class.

ZORI

A traditional type of Japanese footwear, zori, are similar to a Western sandal. Usually made of straw, they have a thong that fits between the large and second toe and over the inside and outside the foot to keep the footwear securely in place. This simple design emerged as a result

Above The modern keikogi, or practice suit, is made from heavyweight cotton.

Above The hakama, or divided skirt, is traditionally blue or black, although high-ranking aikidokas often use other colours.

Left Traditional zori, or straw sandals, are worn to and from the practice tatami, or mat.

of the equirement in Japanese society that one should remove footwear before entering a house. Modern variants are made of rubber or leather and are worn either as fashion accessories or as beachwear.

Above The jo (staff, top) and bokken (wooden sword, bottom) are both traditional aikido weapons.

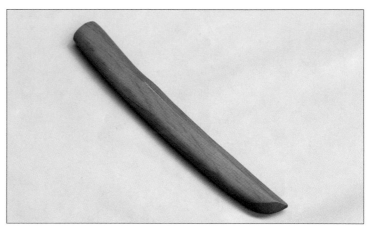

Above The tanto or tanken is a knife used in tanto dori, or knife taking. It is vital to imagine that the blade has the power to cut.

AIKIDO WEAPONS

Shown here are the weapons most commonly used in aikido. The bokken, or bokuto, meaning wooden sword, is approximately the same shape and length as a real Japanese sword. This is used to practise the sword techniques left as a legacy by the founder of the art, which include suburi, or solo exercises; uchikomi, or basic one-step cutting and thrusting with a partner; awase, or basic paired blending practice, and kumitachi, which is a more advanced paired practice that begins to bridge the gap between pure swordsmanship and the practice of aikido. The ultimate practice is tachidori, or sword taking, in which the unarmed aikido exponent faces an attacker who is armed with a sword.

Next is the jo, or short staff. This weapon is approximately 1.25m (4ft) long and 25mm (1in) thick and is used to realize the spearfighting heritage of the art. Disciplines practised include: suburi, or solo exercises; awase, or basic paired blending techniques; kumijo, or advanced paired techniques; and jo tori, techniques for taking a weapon from an attacker. Some aikido schools also practise jo kata, in which imaginary attackers are dealt with in a series of flowing movements. Next down is the tanken, or tanto, which is a wooden knife used to practise defence techniques, using a variety of thrusts, slashes and cuts as if the knife were a small sword or dagger.

HEALTH AND SAFETY

Thankfully in recent years there has been an emphasis on teaching aikido to children, so they can benefit from these new skills and, in the process, ensure the popularity of aikido in years to come. However, with a view to safety, certain techniques should be eliminated from children's practice because of the risk of joint problems occurring in later life. In Britain, for example, children under 14 years of age must practise only with children of a similar age and children aged 14 and above can practise with adults providing that they are segregated within the mat area and a qualified coach is put in charge of the group. Contact any of the international organizations for specific guidance and recommendations (see useful contacts on page 125).

- Another essential for any aikido organization is the recommendation that all aikido instructors who are qualified coaches – and, therefore, able to teach the art unsupervized – should be qualified in basic first aid.

- There should always be a fully stocked first-aid kit readily available and an accident book in which details of any accident can be recorded. There are also formal documents for this purpose.

- Dojo heads should ensure that the building itself is well maintained and in a good state of repair so that it is a safe place in which to practise.

- Objects such as radiators, chairs, wall corners and stanchions should be made safe to avoid injury.

- Tatami (mat) and canvas should be monitored regularly to ensure there are no rips or tears that could snag someone's fingers or toes, and that they are laid properly with no spaces or gaps.

- Any jewellery worn by a student must be taken out or off to avoid harming themselves or others.

- Fingernails should be clean and short, and long hair tied back.

- The practice suit, or keikogi, should be clean and the student must exhibit a high standard of personal hygiene.

- Weapons should be checked for cracks and splinters before every session.

- Dojo heads need to be made aware of any physical or medical problems students may have.

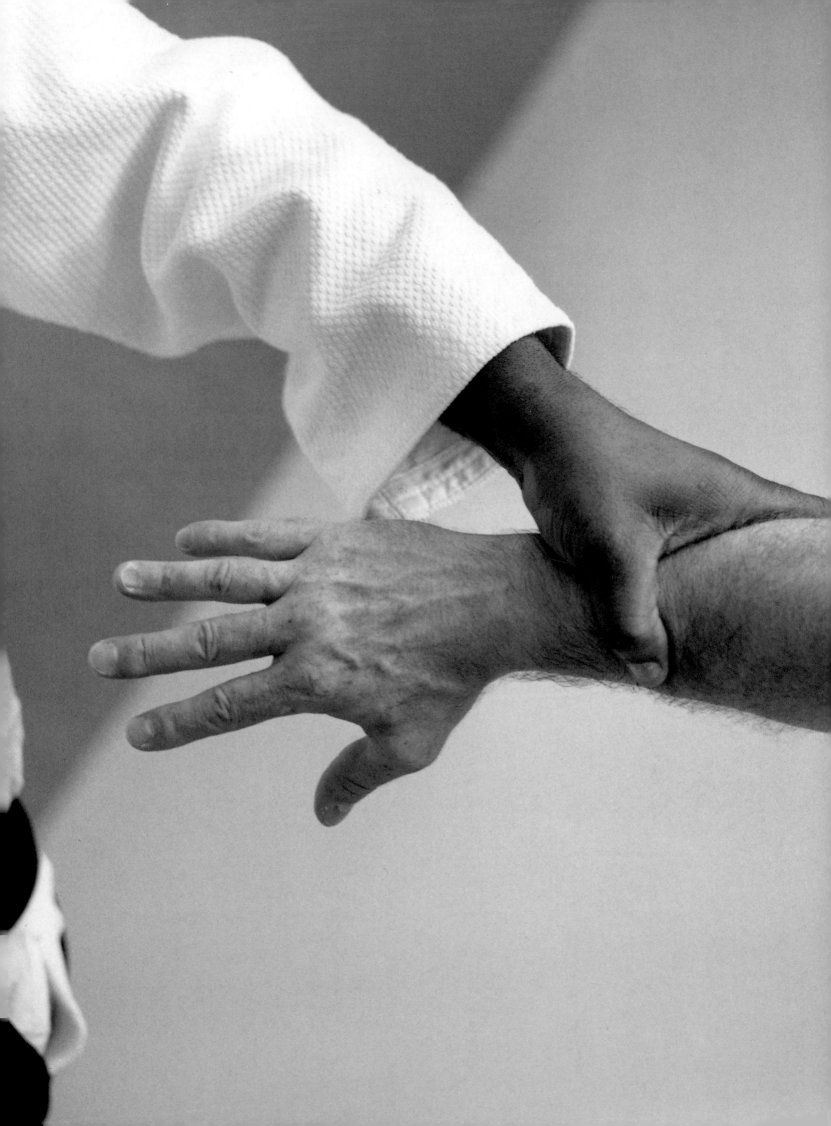

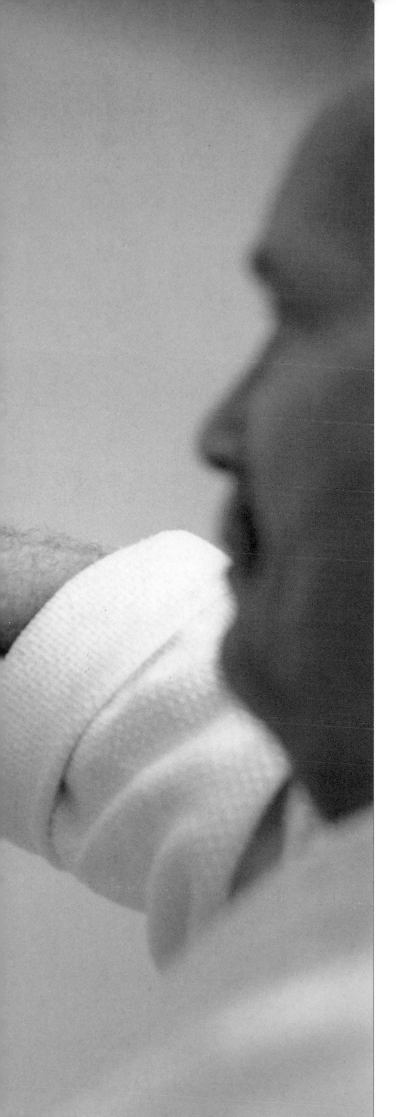

Preparatory Movements

In aikido, as in any other form of physical training, the body has to be prepared. Muscles need warming and gently stretching and the joints need to be put through a range of movements to enable them to accommodate the rigours of practice. What differentiates these exercises from those used in athletics, gymnastics, football and so on is that the mind as well as the body is conditioned. In this section of the book a range of conditioning exercises are set out in the order they are normally taught in the dojo. These exercises, however, are by no means definitive, and you may find that they vary in both form and order depending on which country you are in and, indeed, which region.

Breathing

There is a Chinese saying that breath is the lord of power, and a glance at any of the kung-fu fighting styles dating back to the times of the original Shaolin Temple in AD495 will reveal the great emphasis that was placed on proper and controlled breathing. Followers of the Indian practice of yoga also stress the importance of prana, or breath, and almost any physical endeavour such as aikido can be enhanced by being aware of the difference that controlled breathing can make.

Deep abdominal breathing techniques perform two distinct functions. They imbue the body with oxygen, which relaxes the muscles and prepares them for stretching. They also direct the mind to the tanden in order to develop the mindset necessary to understand the concept of extension of energy from there. During the breathing exercises that follow use the visualization techniques referred to in ki and kokyu (see pages 27–31) as well as the box below.

Inhalation and exhalation

In the illustration to the right, the directional arrows flowing in through the nose show the path of the breath during inhalation. Physically, you need to put your tongue against the roof of your mouth and then inhale through the nose, with the feeling of drawing in purifying energy from the whole universe. Imagine that you are controlling the inhalation of air with the epiglottis at the back of the throat, rather than merely sniffing it in. The breath is then directed (in the mind's eye) to the very top of the head and down the spine to a point about 5cm (2in) below the navel and 5cm (2in) inwards. This is the approximate centre of gravity in the human body and is also regarded as the spiritual centre. Commonly referred to in aikido as the tanden, this point has a similar importance in most of the major doctrines of the Far East. When the breath reaches this point, hold it and imagine that it is coiling up and tensing, in just the same way as a spring would.

The blue directional arrows flowing out through the mouth indicate the path of the exhaled breath. As you start to exhale, contract the cheeks of your bottom (This act, along with the tongue on the roof of the mouth, represents the spiritual closing of the openings of the body.) The breath uncoils in the tanden with a feeling of expansion and follows the same path as the inhalation, but in reverse. The other difference is that the breath that is expelled through the mouth has the quality of emptying all the impurities of the day that have been gathering in the body.

Single-cycle Breathing Exercise 1

All the following breathing exercises follow the same inhalation/exhalation techniques as those outlined opposite. This first single-cycle breathing exercise is one of the more commonly used ones in aikido dojos.

1 To start this exercise, stand in a relaxed position with your feet a shoulder-width apart, hands in front of your thighs with your fingers extended.

2 Inhale as you raise your arms above your head, as if you were cutting up with a sword, to the position shown.

3 Continue inhaling as you lower your arms to shoulder height, palms up. As if pushing up with both hands, raise your body onto the balls of your feet.

4 Turn your hands palms down and effectively swallow your breath. Then begin the exhalation process, with the feeling of pushing down with both hands.

5 Lower your body and feet to the floor gradually and return to the start position, as in step 1, to complete the exercise.

CAUTION

If at any time as you perform these breathing exercises you feel dizzy, faint or see spots of bright light, then stop immediately. These symptoms may indicate problems and you should seek medical advice before continuing.

Single-cycle Breathing Exercise 2

This is a simple breathing exercise that makes you aware of your tanden or centre of gravity. It should be done while imagining cutting up and down with the sword as you raise and then lower your arms.

1 To start this exercise, stand in a relaxed position with your feet a shoulder-width apart, hands slightly to the centre of your body. Always begin breathing exercises by exhaling at the start.

2 Inhale as you raise your arms above your head, as if you were cutting up with a sword, to the position shown.

3 Continue inhaling as you draw your arms down to just above shoulder height. As you do this, make fists with your hands and imagine that you are pulling down a heavy shutter. Hold this position for three seconds.

4 Begin exhaling and allow your arms to relax and slowly return to the start position. Gradually unclench your fists as you feel your tanden expanding.

5 Return to the start position.

Double Inhalation/Exhalation Exercise

This is one of a series of double inhalation/exhalation breathing exercises taught by Tamura Nobuyoshi Sensei from France, perhaps the most senior teacher in Europe and a favourite uke of aikido's founder, Morihei Ueshiba.

1 To start this exercise, stand in a relaxed position with your feet a shoulder-width apart, hands slightly to the centre of your body and with fingers extended.

2 Position your hands just below the navel, palms up, with the fingertips pointing towards each other. As you inhale, draw the hands upwards to the height of your nipples.

3 Turning both hands over, exhale. With a sense of pushing down, extend your hands down to below your navel once more. Try to develop a sense of rhythm and a smooth, uninterrupted movement.

4 This is the hand position of the finished cycle. Prepare to move your right hand across to the side of the hip.

5 Move your right hand across to the side of the hip with the fingers turned inward. As you make a second inhalation, begin a large circular extension with your left hand from the centre line of the body, cutting upwards and outwards. As your hand reaches the apex, pause, then exhale, extending fully outwards until your hand returns to the position in the previous step.

6 From this finish position, begin the same sequence for your other side, swapping hand positions as necessary.

Torifune

Part of misogi, a Shinto purification exercise, torifune is also known as the "rowing exercise". It is used to row spiritually to utopia, or "from this world to the next" in the mind of the practitioner. It is also an excellent way to train to become aware of your tanden.

1 Assume a left hanmi posture, extend the arms and make your hands into fists, with the middle knuckles protruding. Feel as if you are forcefully pushing your arms out with your tanden and shout "Hei!" as you bend your front leg and straighten the back one. Kiai is the expulsion of air caused when you tighten the abdominal muscles.

2 Make sure you pull your arms back with the same intensity used to push them forward. Imagine that you are making two elbow strikes to someone standing behind you. Bear in mind that the energy for this movement comes from the centre of the body in between the hips, just below the navel. As you go back into this position make a kiai shout of "Ho!"

Movement repetitions
Some teachers recommend doing more movement repetitions than others so it really depends on the philosophy of your teacher. Recommended here is doing enough repetitions to last 20 seconds or so.

Side view step 1
This side view allows you to see the depth of the stance in step 1. It is important to have a positive attitude when practising this exercise and to make the kiai shout as loud as is practicable, as the whole idea behind this movement is to summon up an indomitable spirit, gradually increasing in intensity as you perform repetitions.

Side view step 2
This side view of the step 2 posture shows how in this position the front leg is straight and the back leg is bent. The hands are pulled back in a clenched, but relaxed manner onto the front of the pelvic bones. This exercise is normally done at the start of the class and the repetitions for each posture are practised on both the left and the right sides.

Furitama

The accompanying exercise is known as furitama, or "shaking the ball". It is a calming exercise and its purpose is to vibrate energy from your centre to all parts of the body after the vigour and vitality of torifune (see opposite), and is done immediately afterwards.

1 Stand in a relaxed position, feet about a hip-width apart, hands by your sides with fingers extended.

2 Extend the arms out in a large circle above the head with a view to clasping the hands together overhead.

3 Close your eyes and imagine that you are taking in energy from the universe itself as you draw your hands to your tanden or centre of gravity.

4 This picture shows the final position of the hands. From this position the hands are shaken vigorously up and down, at the same time imagining a ball being shaken in your centre. This movement agitates the energy you have received and dissipates it to all extremities of your body. On completion of this exercise, stand as you are with your hands together and mentally fix your gaze between your eyes. Breathe normally. This exercise lasts about 20 seconds in total.

Warm-ups and Stretches

The solo exercises in this section are just a selection of the many available. There is no hard-and-fast rule regarding which warm-up exercises to use and some teachers, depending on their own experience, have created their own. The movements that follow have been recommended by various shihan or master teachers.

The body needs to be warmed sufficiently to avoid any pulls and tears of muscles and ligaments. It is a good idea to practise breathing exercises before you warm up and stretch – this oxygenates the blood that feeds the muscles. Warming up should also increase the heart rate. This will also allow the muscles to stretch by an extra 20 per cent, highly recommended considering the range of sudden stretching that can occur within aikido training. Always be mindful, too, that the warm-ups should aim to mirror the actual training. The exercises shown here condition the back, stomach, hips and knees – all vital elements within training. The wrist exercises in particular stimulate the muscles and tendons of the wrist and forearm in exactly the same way as any aikido technique.

If it is cold you should always perform additional exercises, such as running on the spot or jumping for a couple of minutes, to raise the heart rate more and warm yourself thoroughly before you start stretching. The duration of warm-ups and stretching will depend on your experience. Some aikido organizations emphasize the body conditioning more than others. Generally, though, a reasonable warm-up routine should last 15–20 minutes.

This set of calisthenics is designed to warm the muscles and condition the joints. The exercises include movements adopted by many disciplines as part of their warm-up routines, as well as conditioning exercises that are specific to aikido. Perform all of these exercises with your mind at your centre of gravity.

Muscles and Joints

To avoid injury you must ensure that your muscles are relaxed and warm before you begin stretching in preparation for training. The first exercise stimulates blood flow and wakes up the muscles and joints. Open palms can also be used in a slapping action for the same result.

Stimulating blood flow

Hand detail step 1
You only want to stimulate blood flow and not cause bruising, so note that you strike gently with a half-formed fist, the flat of the fingers making contact rather than the knuckles.

1 Stand with your feet hip-width apart, feet facing forward. Half close your right hand into a fist (see detail) and begin gently striking at your left shoulder, gradually working down the inner and outer arm.

2 After repeating the same procedure for your right shoulder and arm, move on to the upper chest muscles, working down to the abdomen, and inner and outer thighs and calves.

3 Working back up the body, stimulate your buttocks and lower back. Work on your back and the sides of your neck to resolve this part of the exercise. Repeat the movements for 2 minutes.

Twisting upper body

1 Stand naturally, widen your stance so that your feet are a shoulder-width apart and raise and extend your arms.

2 Twist your upper body left and right, pivoting from the hips with your feet facing forward. Begin twisting to the right.

3 In a flowing movement, twist your upper body to the left, keeping your feet facing forward. Repeat for 15 seconds.

Body Stretches

The following are typical body stretches practised in many dojos that follow the traditional art of aikido.

Side stretch

Rotary body stretch

1 With feet apart and a straight back, incline your body to the left with the right arm extended overhead. Exhale.

2 Repeat this movement on the opposite side, this time with your left arm extended. Repeat for 15 seconds.

1 Start with both hands above your head and describe a large circle with your arms, with the tanden as the centre.

2 Be aware of your breathing pattern. Exhale as you go down and inhale as you come up. This is actively harmonizing your breathing with your body movement.

3 Fully extend the arms and touch the mat with your fingertips, if your suppleness will permit. Do not overdo this movement and strain your body.

4 Repeat the movement, describing a circle in the opposite direction. Repeat for 15 seconds.

Back Stretch

If carried out with commitment, this simple back-stretching exercise is an excellent whole-body workout. To avoid injury, work within your abilities and don't take the movements farther than your body will readily allow.

Side views of steps 1 and 2
These two side views show the first part of the exercise from a side-on position, allowing you to see the complete depth of the stretch you should be aiming to achieve. Depending on your degree of suppleness, this could, however, take weeks of daily practice. Don't rush the process.

1 Stand with your legs wider apart than in previous movements, as shown, and with both hands above your head. Bend forward, extending your arms so that your fingers touch the floor. Exhale at the stage. Stroke the floor between your legs, ensuring that the final stroke is farther back than the others.

2 Reversing the movement, extend back up and open your arms wide with your head right back so that you can see the ceiling directly above you. Inhale deeply at this stage.

Hip Rotation

This simple warm-up exercise stretches the central muscles around the hips and waist. In combination with the other warm-up exercises shown here, this sequence helps to prepare the whole body for general aikido techniques.

1 Place your hands on your hips and push your centre forward as far as is comfortable, while keeping your feet flat on the floor.

2 Incline your body to the right, imagining your body is rotating in a circle.

3 Now project your bottom to the rear and straighten your legs as you complete a full circle.

4 Finally, incline your body to your left and complete the circular movement of the whole exercise. Repeat for 20 seconds.

Knee and Calf Bends

These exercises are designed to condition the lower limbs. Aikido can take its toll on the knee joints so it is important to keep them supple. Please take your time with these bends and do only what you can manage.

Knee circles

1 Place your hands on your knees with knees loosely bent and rotate in a circular motion by bending the knees farther forward as they move to the side. You should aim to keep gentle pressure on the front and sides of the joints. This is the basic way, although a variation of this exercise is to open the knees away from one another in to out and out to in.

Calf workout

1 Place your hands on your knees, bend your knees and bring your chest down. Try to keep the soles of your feet flat on the floor. If your knees are stiff, you may have to extend your arms out in front to act as a counterbalance. Otherwise, keep your hands on your knees. As well as exercising the knees, this movement gives your calf muscles a good workout.

Side view for calf workout
This shows the depth of the squat required to stretch the calf muscles fully. Take your time, and as your suppleness grows, deepen the position little by little.

Knee stretch

1 From the start position shown above for the calf workout lower your weight onto one knee, as shown. Make sure that the opposite leg is fully extended and that you make contact with the floor only with the heel of that extended foot. Either extend your arms to maintain your balance or place one hand on your knees and the other on the floor. Hold for five to ten seconds.

2 Repeat for the other leg, again holding the position for five to ten seconds. Do not attempt this exercise if you have a knee problem of any description.

Neck Conditioning

Neck-conditioning exercises are crucial in the preparation of the body. Centre the head between each side-to-side movement and don't rotate it in a complete circle as this can damage the vertebrae and, in some cases, the arteries in the side of the neck.

Neck conditioning 1

1 This first step is simply to turn to the side and look slightly behind while not moving your shoulders.

2 Bring your head back into central alignment momentarily before repeating this movement on the other side. Make sure you keep your shoulders still.

Neck conditioning 2

1 Look upwards and then bring your head down to a central position, hold this momentarily.

2 Now move your head so you are looking downwards, effectively putting your chin on your chest.

Neck conditioning 3

1 Bring your head up again and then, facing directly forward, pick a point on the wall to focus on. While still able to see that point, turn your head to the right.

2 Next, rotate your head downwards in a half circle to the same point on the left side. Repeat steps 1 and 2.

3 Rotate your head in a semicircle from left to right, pausing momentarily, and then right to left. Try to touch your chin on your chest in between movements.

Wrist Flexibility

You must exercise your wrists vigorously, known as tekubi kansetsu junan undo, before every aikido training session. This special emphasis is due to the fact that many of the techniques are directed at the wrists, forearms and elbows.

Nikkyo

1 Place one hand over the back of the other, as shown, and with a curling motion draw the hand back towards your chest. This flexes the wrist and also conditions the back of the hand.

2 In this position you can see the hand fully drawn back and at maximum stretch.

Sankyo

1–3 These three images show the conditioning exercise for a technique called sankyo. Take your hand, as shown here, and using a type of wringing action, stretch the wrist outwards, away from the body.

Kote gaeshi

1–2 For this conditioning exercise take your hand in the other and twist it inwards and downwards in front of your body. Imagine that your mind is a high-pressure water jet blasting up your body from your centre and through the arms and fingers.

Basic Movements

This section introduces the hanmi stance and deals with the basic aikido body movements: tandoku dosa, solo exercises, and sotai dosa, exercises with a partner. Tandoku dosa teaches the student how to stand up properly and, using certain body motions, how to distribute their weight to allow rapid movement in any direction. In sotai dosa you are able to test your stability and "centredness" with a partner holding you strongly to enable you to learn to displace your partner's balance without recourse to physical strength.

USING THE TANDEN

A student first has to become aware of the tanden, or centre of gravity (see page 31). Doing this is largely a spiritual exercise where breathing techniques and a strong imagination play an important part. Initially, one has to learn to contemplate this centre in a quiet environment. It is much more difficult to "keep centred" when moving around.

Hanmi is the basic kamae, or posture, that the aikido practitioner assumes in which they stand as if holding a Japanese sword. The bokken, or wooden sword, is held in the same way as in kendo, and the difference lies in the kamae. Kendo and its subordinate art iaido, or way of drawing the sword, involve the feet pointing directly forwards, parallel to each other. Hanmi involves positioning the feet apart with the back foot pointing outwards at approximately 60 degrees to the forward foot. Tandoku dosa, or solo training, helps the student to move from the centre. One learns that the centre moves first and then the body follows. Sotai dosa is a more advanced level where the student learns to move in a centred way, while also dealing with another person holding with full strength.

Hanmi

This is the basic stance of aikido and is called hanmi, which means "half stance". This is a reference to the angle the body assumes in relation to an attacker – about 45 degrees to the front.

Hidari (left) hanmi

Turning at 45 degrees to an attacker, your feet assume the back triangle stance, or ura sankaku. Hold your hands as if you were gripping a Japanese sword (though with fingers extended), with, in this case of left hanmi, the left hand at approximately the height of the solar plexus and the other at the height of the navel.

Migi (right) hanmi

This right hanmi posture shows how with 60 to 70 per cent of your body weight on the front foot, and the back foot at an angle of approximately 60 degrees to the front foot, this is an extremely versatile posture that permits rapid movement in any direction.

Tandoku Dosa

These solo exercises are unique to aikido and involve repetition of the art's core movements. Their aim is to teach you to move your body evasively while maintaining hanmi, or the half-stance posture (see opposite).

This is where you first become aware of the importance of maintaining a stable posture and of the centre line of the body, and its role in moving you out of the line of an attack.

The following movements occur naturally in the techniques themselves but here they are taken out of context so that you can practise them until they become second nature.

Irimi ashi: tsugi ashi

1 This is the right hanmi posture. From here the idea is to push forward off the back foot with both feet, gliding across the surface of the floor and advancing across the dojo in the same right posture. The back foot follows behind.

2 The back foot has followed up closely behind the front foot and the whole movement is about to start again. At this stage the knees are slightly bent and the hands and forearms are extended as if cutting upwards with two sword blades.

3 Perform continuously until you reach the other side of the dojo, where you make tenkai ashi (a 180-degree pivot) on the balls of your feet. Continue until you get back to where you started from.

Irimi ashi: ayumi ashi

1 As before, the posture is right hanmi, but this time the back foot comes forward in the same way as it does for normal walking. It is important to practise repetitions in both postures.

2 The body weight starts to transfer from the right to the left foot as the left foot comes forward. Keep the balls of both feet in contact with the floor for stability and to move off the attacking line.

3 With left foot forward, the student is in left hanmi and ready to bring the right foot forward to repeat the movement on the other side. Practise this up and down the dojo, turning in tenkai ashi each end.

Tenkan ashi

1 Start in the hanmi stance, as shown here, and prepare for the tenkan, or turning movement, which is one of the cornerstones of aikido.

2 Pivoting on the front foot by 180 degrees, pass through the kaiten, or rotation movement. Keep the ball of your rear foot in contact with the floor at all times.

3 By drawing the right foot circularly back the student faces the opposite direction to where he started. It is important to keep your weight on your front foot.

Kaiten ashi

Tenkan

The tenkan, or turning movement, is one of the cornerstones of aikido. It involves passing through the kaiten movement shown to the left and pivoting on the front foot by 180 degrees, remembering to keep the ball of your rear foot in light contact with the floor at all times.

Irimi tenkan

For irimi tenkan, take a large step forward, as shown in irimi in step 1 on page 49, before making the pivot described here. For irimi tenkan where you enter with the back foot, step forward with the back foot and then perform the pivot.

1 Pictured here is the kaiten, or rotation movement. From the hanmi stance, step off the central line – the imaginary line of an attack that is aimed at the centre of your body, whether the face or the stomach – with your leading foot.

2 As you place that foot, rotate your hips so that your body is now facing in the same direction as the attack. Your left hand here is used not to block any movement, but to parry or deflect it. The idea is to get behind the attack and allow it to carry on.

Shikko

Unique to aikido, shikko, also known as samurai knee walking, derives from Japan's feudal history where there were no chairs, and all social activity – doing business. eating a meal or sitting in conversation – was carried out in the formal kneeling position known as seiza.

A samurai had to be ready for sudden attack, even while seated, and although etiquette meant that he had to surrender his katana, or long sword, at the door of a host's house before entering, he was entitled to retain his kodachi, or short sword. Defence from a kneeling position with a sword was one of the samurai's essential skills. Called iai jutsu, or the art of fast sword drawing, it enabled an exponent to react swiftly to sudden aggression, very often cutting down an assailant without even having to stand up. The knee movements first used in this way form the basis of samurai walking in aikido.

Physically, shikko is also very beneficial, exercising many parts of the body at the same time – the waist and hips, knees, ankles and toes are all stimulated. By far the most important reason for practising shikko is to become aware of the importance of using your hips and your body's centre of gravity, or tanden, to facilitate economy of movement. Because you do not have the same mobility on your knees as you do on your feet, if you can perform techniques well on your knees, the improvement in your standing techniques becomes more marked.

1 Start in right hanmi position, with your weight on the toes and knee of your left leg, incline your weight forward and go down onto the right knee.

2 Swivelling forward on that right knee, and with a strong hip movement, bring your left knee forward while keeping both feet together, as shown here.

3 Place your left knee on the floor and begin the whole motion again, swivelling on your left knee this time. Ensure that each forward motion originates from the hips and that you maintain the defensive position of the hands: in other words, make sure that your leading hand is the same as your leading knee.

Sotai Dosa

In paired exercises you are able to test your stability and "centredness" with a partner holding you strongly (usually by the wrists), the aim being to learn to displace your partner's centre and, therefore, balance, with a variety of extension techniques.

Sotai dosa are paired exercises designed to familiarize you with aikido movements. In the basic exercises shown here, learn how to move your partner's body using kokyu, or breath power, as opposed to strength, as well as move off the centre line of your partner's attack. These exercises vary from school to school, but the principles are the same. This sequence shows the gyaku hanmi katate-dori irimi exercise practised at jodan (upper level), chudan (middle level) and gedan (lower level).

Gyaku hanmi katate-dori

In this starting position the uke holds his partner's wrist and tries to keep the grip all the way through the movement.

Irimi jodan

This exercise moves your partner's centre of gravity without recourse to physical strength. Tori steps forward with the leading foot and pushes off with the back foot. The same entering movement is used at three levels – jodan (upper), chudan (middle) and gedan (lower). These are selected according to whether your opponent is taller, the same size or smaller than you. The levels also show the motion to deal with an attack to the head, to the midsection and below the belt. Here (left) tori cuts upwards while bending his front knee and leaning his gravity into the cutting motion. Uke is driven away with great force. He maintains a strong grip, but relaxes his shoulders to harmonize with the force rather than resisting it.

Chudan

From the starting position the same movement is repeated, but now tori enters with his extension at chudan or middle level.

Gedan

From the starting position the same movement is repeated, but now tori enters with his hands at the gedan or lower level.

Kaiten

Kaiten is a movement used to deflect an opponent's energy sideways. Tori steps slightly to his right, then turns his hips leftwards, deflecting uke's power.

Uchi kaiten

1 From the starting position tori cuts upwards with a spiral motion to raise uke's elbow, entering slightly with his forward foot.

2 Tori then enters with his back leg passing inside underneath uke's arm.

3 With a sharp turn of the hips tori cuts downwards, projecting uke's elbow forward and causing loss of balance. Tori needs to cut with the gripped arm as if it were a sword. This extension causes uke's raised elbow to project forward and takes away his capacity to generate strength.

Gyaku hanmi katate-dori tenkan ho

This is the reverse-stance one-handed-grip turning movement, which is also called the tenkan, and is one of the most fundamental movements in aikido. The successful execution of the body-turning motions shown here rely on understanding the mechanics of the movement and also keeping aware of your centre of gravity, the tanden.

1 With your right hand, take your partner's left wrist, or vice versa. Incline your body weight forward, thus establishing good contact with your partner's extended energy.

2 Turning your hips to the right, drop your bodyweight on to your partner's grip. Imagine you are uniting with his power. Pivot on your leading foot and draw the rear foot 180 degrees to the back of your partner.

3 Extend the hand that is being held forward and your free hand as well. This creates the feeling that energy is being extended from your tanden and that your body is working as a whole unit.

Ai hanmi katate-dori irimi

Illustrated here is ai hanmi katate-dori irimi, a one-handed mutual-stance entering step. In ai hanmi the contact is right hand to right hand, or vice versa. This sequence shows tori entering with the forward foot, keeping his back foot in balance with his partner's. Some schools call this attack kosa dori, meaning a crossed-hands grip. This movement is not so practically relevant to a contemporary fighting context, and originates from the fact that both ai hanmi and gyaku hanmi wrist attacks were used in many of the old grappling arts. It is important for uke to try and maintain a flexible grip throughout these exercises.

1 Your right wrist is gripped by your partner's right hand.

2 (first variation) As you step forward with your right foot, raise your right arm, as if you are cutting upwards with a sword and then push forward with your centre. This is irimi with the leading foot in front of uke.

2 (second variation) Place your left hand on the attacker's neck or shoulder and pull her backwards slightly, taking her balance. Then extend your sword arm to weaken the attacker's grip. This is the classic shikaku, or blind spot position, in which uke's back is directly in front of tori's chest. This is irimi made with the rear foot coming forward and behind uke.

Ai hanmi uchi kaiten

This movement is known as an uchi kaiten, or inward rotary exercise. Shown here is ai hanmi when both uke and tori are in a right hanmi stance. It involves rotating inside and underneath uke's arm. Tori's attitude when cutting up with her right hand is that the underside of her hand and arm is the cutting edge of a sword. Tori does not lift her hand to raise uke's arm, but leans her body weight into the cutting-up motion. This provides far more power than just muscular strength.

1 In this situation, the uke (the person receiving the technique) is attacking the wrist of the tori (the person delivering the technique).

2 Tori steps in with her right foot and raises her hands as if cutting upward with a sword. Tori's left hand is here shown inside uke's right arm.

3 She steps under the uke's raised arm and rotates her body inwards with a turn of her hips. At the same time she pushes down on the uke's arm, as if cutting downwards with a sword.

Irimi issoku

This routine involves entering with one step into the side of your partner. The attack here is gyaku hanmi katate-dori, but this movement can be adapted to any attack and serves two purposes: to enter into the attacker's shikaku, or blind spot, neutralizing the attack; and to disengage the attacker's grip.

1 As your partner grabs you by your right wrist, resist the temptation to pull your hand back.

2 Instead, enter with your right foot and rotate your hand in a spiralling movement. Using your left hand to cut off his remaining grip, enter deeply behind him.

3 In this final position you are in your partner's shikaku, or blind spot. From here it is possible to execute a wide variety of disabling techniques.

Ukemi

Literally defined as "the art of falling", as in a forward or backward roll, ukemi is probably the first thing that you will be taught how to do when you join an aikido club. The reason for this is that you must learn how to neutralize the effects of aikido techniques and build up the confidence necessary to fall to the floor without injuring yourself. Only by doing this will you be able to learn the art and so make progress.

The concept behind ukemi is actually a lot deeper than this rather simplistic explanation implies, and it can more appropriately be described as "the art of recovery". This is because every technique applied on you in aikido requires you either to neutralize or recover from it – this principle is true no matter what situation you have been put in – be it a throw, an arm lock or a pinning technique. Being able to recover, or take ukemi, is central to learning aikido, because when techniques are applied with full commitment they can be dangerous if the practitioner cannot take ukemi.

Mae Ukemi

This sequence demonstrates the mae ukemi, or forward roll. It is a basic movement in aikido that will help to ensure your safety from the outset. All ukemi techniques require making your body as free of tension as you can, here achieved by losing your balance into the roll.

1 In the start position for the front roll, place the little finger of your hand on the tatami (mat), and adopt an attitude of extending yourself forward.

2 From the front foot, push off and roll along your leading arm, diagonally across your back and then up the other arm. As you push yourself forward, adopt an attitude of losing your balance into the roll, rather than mechanically placing yourself in it. In this way you are "recovering" from the situation.

3 This is the position you are in as you come out of the roll. When performed correctly, it will involve contact with the outside muscles of your arms, shoulder, back and leg, and it acts almost as a body massage. As a result, at the end of a practice you should be enjoying a feeling of well-being, though the function of the movement is, perhaps, one day to save your life.

Ushiro Ukemi

This sequence demonstrates the ushiro ukemi, or backward roll. Again, as with mae ukemi, aim for an attitude of actually losing your balance into the roll so that you create the feeling of recovering it again. This prevents you becoming too mechanical and tense.

1 Stand as shown, with one foot behind the other and your arms extended out in front of your body.

2 Lower your weight onto the outside of your calf muscle (not your knee), and project your bottom out as if making yourself into a ball.

3 Roll back onto your outer thigh and diagonally across your back, kicking your legs over your shoulder. It is important to tuck your chin in as you roll. This keeps your head off the mat and ensures that you roll across the back of your shoulders and end up on the same leg as when you started.

4 During this movement, your body should make contact with the floor as it did for mae ukemi, but this time in reverse order – leg, back, shoulder and finally your arm.

5 This is the position adopted after the roll and prior to the standing up position shown in step 1.

Aikido
Techniques

There are literally hundreds of techniques within the framework of aikido, and in a book of this scope it is only possible to show some of them. Because the art of aikido is based on certain core principles, it is possible to interpret instructions in a variety of ways. It is wise to be wary of an instructor who says that there is only one way to do things because as long as something makes sense within the framework of aikido, it is likely to work. The one thing most true aikidokas attempt to relinquish through their training is their ego. Included in this section are some of the classic attacks within the aikido repertoire. Some styles are more martial than others and feature strong attacks, while others modify the intensity and are used more as a medium of contact between partners to facilitate the practice of technique.

Striking Methods

The following techniques are the basic strikes most commonly used in aikido. They are taken from classical Japanese attacks with the sword, spear and knife rather than contemporary fighting attacks. All attacks in aikido – even a grip on the wrist – are made with full commitment. Without this, the techniques cannot be practised. This is because without a committed, spirited attack there is no force to harmonize with, no energy to deflect – quite simply, no aikido!

Aikido techniques are executed when two partners come together and a contact is established. When that contact is ai hanmi, both partners have the same foot forward – right foot to right foot. When the contact is gyaku hanmi, the partners have their opposite feet forward – right foot to left foot. This idea permeates all aikido technique in that as the attacks become more advanced the postures of both partners remain the same. Let us take the example of shomen-uchi, a strike to the front of the head with the blade of the hand (see below).

As contact is made, the partners end up in the same posture as in ai hanmi katate-dori. Conversely, yokomen-uchi is a similar strike, but the target is the side of the head. As contact is made here, both partners come together in gyaku hanmi. This principle applies to every technique and is the main reason why ai hanmi and gyaku hanmi techniques constitute the majority of what is practised in a typical dojo. Repetitive training in basic technique from these two postures, therefore, prepares practitioners for more advanced training.

Shomen-uchi

This first sequence of images is shomen-uchi, or front-head strike, based on the basic overhead cut with a Japanese sword. Tori protects his head against a possible thrust to his face, prior to extending his handblade in a large circle towards the front of uke's head.

1 As its name suggests, this attack is made with the blade of the hand held as if it were a sword striking the centre of uke's head.

2 Tori brings his feet together while simultaneously protecting his face.

3 As he steps onto his right foot, he launches the attack. This all happens in one flowing motion, with the strike quickly executed and aimed above the target as if cutting on the backstroke in the same way as a sword. You should adopt the feeling of "cutting" and not "hitting" the target.

Yokomen-uchi

This sequence of images shows yokomen-uchi, or side head strike. Steps 1 and 2 for shomen-uchi (see opposite) are repeated; however step 3, instead of aiming above the target, aims the cut circularly at the side of uke's head/neck. The power here is generated by a hip turn.

1 This attack begins in the same way as shomen-uchi, with the blade of the left hand held as if it were a sword, but this time the strike is slightly diagonal to the side of the head or neck.

2 Tori brings his feet together while simultaneously protecting his face with his right hand.

3 As he steps onto his right foot, tori launches the attack. This happens in one flowing motion, and the strike is executed quickly, aimed to the side of the head or upper neck. Adopt the feeling of "cutting" and not "hitting" the target.

Chudan Tsuki

The middle thrust, or chudan tsuki, is a modern punching technique. The original punching style was based on a knife thrust to the midsection called furizuki, or upward circular thrust, performed as if holding a knife and hiding it, and then striking towards the solar plexus.

1 This attack begins in the same way as shomen-uchi, with the blade of the left hand held as if it were a sword. The punching fist is held underneath the right ribcage with the shoulder pulled in.

2 Tori brings his feet together, extending his left hand as a protection against an attack.

3 As he steps on to his right foot, tori launches the attack in one flowing motion, with the strike executed quickly. As the forward step with the right foot is made, the left hand pulls back and the right fist travels out.

Chudan tsuki thrust
When tori's attacking arm is two-thirds extended (the stage shown between step 2 and step 3), the wrist rotates sharply so that the right-hand palm is face down. Step 3 illustrates how the impact is made with the knuckles of the index and third fingers and the fist makes contact at the area between the left and right ribs, just below the breastbone. The power of the punch is generated by a turn of the hips.

Grabbing Techniques

Shown below are some of the classic grabbing attacks. The attitude when grabbing should be one of trying to control your partner's whole body. It is also important to attack off the centre line of your partner, positioning yourself so you are difficult to hit.

Ai hanmi katate-dori

Also called kosa-dori, this is a mutual-stance one-hand hold. Both uke (the person receiving) and tori (the person delivering) are in the same stance and making contact with the same hand left to left, or right to right).

Gyaku hanmi katate-dori

Here uke and tori assume an opposite, or reverse, posture to each other. Contact is made with opposite hands (right hand to left). Uke must grip with the little finger first quite strongly, then each successive finger with a little less power.

Sode-dori

In this attack called sode-dori, or sleeve grab, uke grasps tori's sleeve. It is a more practical attack than the wrist grips already shown here, and gives tori an opportunity to practise the same techniques as in gyaku hanmi.

Kata-dori

Uke grabs tori at the shoulder in kata-dori, or shoulder grab. The contact is the same as in gyaku hanmi (see above), so this attack enables training in the techniques from that posture. Uke can attack with a free foot or hand, and so tori must move off that line of attack and out of danger as a defence technique is applied.

Morote-dori

Uke grips tori's wrist with both hands in morote-dori, or two hands holding one wrist. From tori's perspective, although the stance is gyaku hanmi (see above), it is possible to practise both ai hanmi and gyaku hanmi style techniques because there are now two hands to choose between.

Rear-attack Techniques

Some of the simpler rear-attack techniques, or ushirowaza, can be taught at a beginner or intermediate level, but the majority are for intermediate to advanced training. Traditionally, ushirowaza techniques begin with uke and tori in ai hanmi stance with their hands crossed and fingertips pointing at each other's eyes (see step 1 below). This equates to the position in aikido swordsmanship of seigan, or crossed swords pointing at the eyes. The most basic attack is uke gripping both of tori's wrists from behind (ushiro ryote-dori) as shown below.

Always remain aware of your tanden when practising ushirowaza. This ensures that you are as stable as possible and that your balance is difficult to disturb. Constant tanden awareness also means that you can extend your energy forwards, essential in the execution of many techniques from this attack, as your body actually moves backwards. Practising renzoku uchikomi, or continuous stepping and striking practice, with a partner in aiki ken (aikido swordsmanship), up and down the dojo, is an excellent way of understanding this concept (see pages 102–3).

There are many techniques within ushirowaza. In ushiro ryo sode-dori both sleeves are gripped; in ushiro ryo hijitori both elbows are gripped; in ushiro ryo kata-dori both shoulders are gripped; in ushiro katate-dori kube-shime one wrist is gripped while a choke hold is applied with the other arm; and in ushiro munedakishime a bear hug is applied from behind. All of these movements begin from the crossed-hand position below. The attacker never approaches from behind. Virtually all aikido techniques can be practised from ushiro attacks.

Crossing hands

1 In this posture, uke and tori are in ai hanmi stance (see page 54) crossing hands as if they were two swords. This is the classical beginning of all ushirowaza, or techniques from attacks to the rear.

Entering behind

2 Here uke cuts tori's arm down with his leading swordhand, gripping the wrist at the same time and moving the balance forwards. This makes it easier for uke to advance round the back of tori.

Ushiro ryote-dori

3 Uke takes a large step with the rear foot around the back of tori and grabs the other wrist. The aim is to grasp the other wrist and immobilize tori's arms. In the original grappling arts the intent would be to pull the arms back together and strike the centre of the spine with the knee causing damage. The most basic of the ushirowaza attacks, ushiro ryote-dori, or two hands on two hands from behind, is also known as ushiro tekubi tori, behind wrist hold.

Applying the Techniques

The diversity that exists when it comes to the application of aikido techniques can be confusing for new students. However, no matter what style of instruction aikido teachers adopt, all are united by the principles that the founder taught. On the next few pages there follows a selection of techniques picked from the hundreds available, and these include many of the classic attacks in the aikido repertoire.

As well as the variety of teaching styles, dependent on the perspective of the individual teacher, aikido has techniques that are large and flowing as well as those that are short and sharp. Add to this the fact that there are both traditional and non-traditional forms of the art and it makes you realize the variation that is out there. The techniques that follow represent only a fraction of what is available. Some of the techniques are in omote form, which means movements initially towards the front of an attacker, and others are in ura form which are movements towards the back of an attacker. These concepts roughly equate to irimi and tenkan, or entering and turning in relation to your partner.

SWORDSMANSHIP WITHOUT THE SWORD

This phrase is sometimes used to describe the rationale behind aikido techniques. Whether you are an advocate of weapons or not, it is plain to see that when you execute the various thrusting, spiral and circular arm and body movements they are based on the same movements found in Japanese swordsmanship (also, to a lesser extent, in Japanese spearfighting, as typified by the jo). So when looking at the techniques on the following pages look carefully at the postures, arm movements and positions and if you place an imaginary bokken (wooden sword) or jo in the hands of tori – the person executing the technique – you will often see the relevance of the actions.

Suwariwaza Kata-dori Ikkyo Omote

Suwariwaza, or seated techniques, are a throwback to old Japan when business was conducted in the seated seiza position. Defence techniques were developed to counter attacks to someone in seiza by either an armed or unarmed aggressor.

1 Uke attacks using a kata-dori (shoulder grab). Tori and uke are in gyaku hanmi, or reverse posture, in relation to one another. Uke positions himself as he grabs tori's shoulder so that he must take one step forward in order to be able to strike tori with the other hand. This is the correct ma-ai or combative distance. Tori needs to move as if he were going to be hit with uke's free hand.

2 Tori moves his body to the side with shikko (knee walking), stretching his right arm outwards and cutting down on uke's arm with his left, causing him to lose balance.

3 Tori takes uke's wrist, pressing it against his right shoulder. Simultaneously, tori enters into uke's side, applying handblade pressure to uke's elbow.

4 Entering by stepping forward with his right leg, tori controls uke's elbow and pushes him down with power from the hips. It is important to relax the shoulders and move from your centre.

5 Tori pins uke's arm and wrist with power from his tanden, or centre of gravity. Always pin uke's arm higher than 90 degrees to the body. This is to prevent uke gaining leverage to resist.

Suwariwaza Shomen-uchi Irimi-nage Ura

This seated front-head-strike technique encapsulates the idea of harmonizing with an attack, neutralizing it, and then applying defence. Throughout the movement tori is a whirlwind in the centre of the action, sending uke spinning around his centre of gravity.

1 Uke and tori start this sequence in hanmi when uke and tori face each other in a half stance or 45 degrees to each other.

2 Uke enters with his rear foot and makes a shomen-uchi strike. Tori enters with his rear foot and deflects with his sword arm, gripping uke's collar.

3 Tori continues to turn, swivelling on his knee and dissipating uke's energy. At this stage tori and uke are facing the same direction.

4 Tori withdraws his right foot in a circular move and drops his weight on the collar grip made in step 2. Uke follows trying to retain his balance.

5 Tori reverses his stance and body weight by swivelling on his right knee and raising his left leg. Then, withdrawing his left knee, tori projects uke to the mat.

6 Restraining uke's neck with his left handblade, tori uses his right hand to control uke's free arm.

Suwariwaza Shomen-uchi Kote-gaeshi

The actual body movement of this front-head-strike technique is almost identical to irimi-nage. The focus now, however, is on uke's wrist. The idea is to place your hand on the back of his as a perfect match and to turn it sharply outwards and downwards.

1 Uke (the person receiving the technique) and tori (the person delivering the technique) start off in hanmi.

2 Uke attacks with shomen-uchi, or a front-head strike, and tori deflects the strike with his sword arm.

3 Tori simultaneously takes uke's wrist with his left hand. This enables tori to control uke's hand prior to tori placing his other hand on the back of uke's hand. Tori extends power from his tanden, making it impossible for uke to lift his arm.

4 Placing his hand on the back of uke's wrist, tori swivels on his right knee and applies pressure on uke's wrist, causing him to fall to the mat. The sudden inward twisting of uke's hand causes uke's wrist to buckle – the discomfort he feels makes him lean forward to compensate and therefore he loses his balance. Uke must harmonize with tori.

5 Tori applies strong pressure on the back of uke's elbow and, maintaining the grip with his left hand, forces uke to spin over onto his front.

6 Tori applies an immobilizing pin with both arms. This is done by tori hugging uke's arm against his body, the lower arm just below uke's elbow and the upper arm gripping uke's wrist. Pressure is applied by a total body turn towards uke's head – this can result in dislocation of the shoulder joint if applied too hard.

Hanmi Handachi Shiho-nage Ura

Hanmi handachi techniques involve one sitting and one standing, practised to simulate tori dealing with a taller opponent. The technique here is shiho-nage, or four-corner throw from behind. The principle is to fold the attacker in half to bring him down to your size.

1 Uke and tori start off in hanmi handachi with tori sitting and uke standing. The full name for this position is gyaku hanmi katate-dori, or one-handed grip.

2 Tori makes a tenkan movement, cutting forward with her sword arm to take uke's balance.

3 Tori cuts upwards and enters under uke's arm, simultaneously taking uke's wrist with her other hand.

4 With a strong turn of the hip, tori swivels on her left knee and cuts down the centre line of her body with both of her hands holding uke's wrist.

5 Entering deeply behind uke, tori drops onto her right knee and pins uke's wrist, as shown.

Hanmi Handachi Uchi Kaiten-nage

This is an example of the rotary or spin throw with one sitting and one standing. The idea is for tori to spin uke onto his back and not to throw him into a forward roll. Uke manipulates his own body to roll to safety in a kind of half forward, half sideways ukemi.

1 Uke and tori begin this sequence in hanmi handachi.

2 Tori raises uke's elbow by cutting upwards with her gripped hand in a kind of spiral motion. Having raised uke's elbow and broken the power of his grip, tori then enters underneath his arm.

3 Drawing uke's arm back, tori keeps uke's head down with her left hand.

4 Tori grips uke's left wrist with her right hand from underneath while maintaining the pressure on uke's neck. At this stage tori is not throwing uke directly forward – the idea is to spin him onto his back so tori is extending across uke's body.

5 Stepping forward with a strong turn of the hip, tori throws uke with a spinning motion – this is achieved in the following way. Tori's right hand, while still being held, cuts upwards from underneath and takes a strong grip on uke's arm. While keeping uke's head down with her left hand, tori then enters with her right foot onto her right knee in shikko, or knee walk, driving forcefully with her right hip. By tori extending her right arm, uke's arm is pushed forward creating pressure on his shoulder from which ukemi is the only answer.

Hanmi Handachi Yokomen-uchi Shiho-nage

Yokomen-uchi, or side-head strike, features a strike to the side of tori's head with the handblade. There is no block involved. Tori extends his arms to meet uke's attack and harmonize with the movement. Then uke's attack is neutralized and her balance extended forward.

1 Uke and tori start here in hanmi handachi. Uke attacks in a circular motion and tori moves off the attacking line inside of uke's motion. Tori extends his arms as if raising a sword to parry an attack.

2 As uke attacks with yokomen-uchi, or side head strike, the target of which is the side of the head, tori moves in a circular fashion inside the strike, parrying with his left sword arm and trapping uke's attacking arm, drawing her balance towards him.

3 Tori raises uke's arm by cutting up in a spiral as if raising a sword. Then, controlling uke's wrist with both hands, tori enters under the arm with his rear foot and, swivelling 180 degrees on his left knee, cuts down.

4 Now, facing uke, tori enters with his right foot dropping onto his knee. Cutting down as if with a sword, tori destroys uke's balance as she begins to topple back.

5 The final pinning position. Tori pins uke's wrist to the floor, with his body weight ensuring that there is no gap between uke's elbow and her head. In the original jujutsu form the technique would include a finishing blow to the head.

Ai Hanmi Katate-dori Shiho-nage Omote

The most basic way to practise this one-hand grab technique, this represents the principle of cutting up and down with a sword. From the initial grab tori cuts across uke's belly with a sword, steps in while raising the sword, turns by 180 degrees and cuts down again.

1 Uke starts this attack by grabbing tori's right wrist with ai hanmi katate-dori, or a mutual-stance one-handed grab.

2 Tori takes uke's wrist and, reinforcing with the left hand, deflects uke's energy sideways. Because tori stretches uke's arm in front of him and to the side, a dead side is created so that uke cannot retaliate in any way.

3 Tori steps forward with his back leg and raises uke's arm as if raising a sword. This causes stress on uke's wrist which he cannot resist and facilitates tori's movement underneath uke's arm.

4 By turning 180 degrees with a powerful twist of the hip, tori controls uke's elbow and wrist, causing him to lose his balance backwards.

5 As if cutting down with a sword, tori leans his centre of gravity forward and takes control of uke with strong pressure on his wrist and elbow.

Step 5 pinning technique

When applying the final pinning movement, don't allow any gap between uke's elbow and his head. If there is a gap then uke can generate more power to resist the pinning effect and potentially wriggle out of the grab.

Gyaku Hanmi Uchi Kaiten-nage Omote

This is a basic way of doing this inward rotary throw technique and is another good example of the idea of cutting up and down in the same way as with a sword. It is vital for tori to push forward with the elbow as he cuts upwards, otherwise uke will be able to stop him.

1 Uke begins this sequence by attacking tori with gyaku hanmi katate-dori. This is when uke and tori are in reverse postures and uke is gripping tori's wrist with one hand.

2 Tori raises uke's elbow by cutting upwards with his arm, as if raising a sword. This takes away uke's capacity to generate strength in that arm and enables tori to slip underneath it.

3 Tori steps under uke's raised arm with his rear leg and applies a strong hip turn, cutting forwards across uke's body.

4 Stepping back with his right leg and cutting low to the floor, tori takes uke's left wrist and, with his left hand, prevents uke from standing up.

Step 4 firm control
In step 4, keep uke's head under control with your centre of gravity rather than with upper-arm strength.

5 Entering with his whole body and turning his hips, tori extends his right arm and exerts pressure on uke's left shoulder. As tori is already controlling uke's head, uke's body is compelled to spin onto his back. Rather than crash onto his back uke extends himself half forwards, half sideways and takes ukemi, rolling out of danger.

Ai Hanmi Katate-dori Udegarami-nage Omote

This one-hand grab technique begins like the ikkyo arm pin, taking uke down prior to the throw. As he does this, tori takes his own wrist for added power. Uke's wrist control and body position are very similar to shiho-nage but the effect is amplified by the arm twining.

1 Here we see uke attacking tori with ai hanmi katate-dori, or mutal-stance one-hand grab (see page 54).

2 Tori cuts upwards with his right sword hand while controlling uke's right elbow with his left. So, with his held right hand tori uses his handblade to cut into uke's wrist, breaking his grip. This raises uke's elbow, which tori takes with his left hand and then steps in and drops his weight onto uke's elbow.

3 Tori steps in deeply towards uke's armpit with his left foot. While uke is low down, tori takes his own right wrist with his left hand prior to the entering movement of the next stage.

4 Tori takes a sweeping, circular step with his right foot around the front of uke with the attitude of hitting his face with his own hand.

5 Tori makes a tenkan movement with his right foot and applies pressure to uke's arm. Here tenkan, or a turning movement, is shown from steps 4–5 as tori steps in front of uke and makes a 180-degree turn on his right foot. This has the effect of forcing him downwards where tori can finally control his arm by his head.

6 This is the final pinning position of the technique. Uke's wrist and elbow are bent (see box to right). Tori extends his two hands away from himself, causing uke to submit.

Ai hanmi katate-dori pin
The pin shown here is similar to that for shiho-nage, except that both hands are used. Tori's left hand grabs his own right wrist for added leverage and power. Tori extends downwards, exerting strong pressure on uke's wrist and elbow.

Gyaku Hanmi Irimi-nage Ura

This is a basic way to do the entering throw from a reverse-stance one-hand grip. Tori disengages the grip and enters behind uke into the shikaku, or blind spot. The priority is to keep turning, staying in the centre of the action, with uke spinning around tori's centre.

1 Uke attacks with a wrist grab in gyaku hanmi katate-dori, or reverse stance one-hand grab.

2 Tori disengages uke's hand. To do this, tori rotates his gripped left hand/wrist inwards and at the same time cuts off the remnants of that grip with his right handblade. Tori then enters deep behind uke using the irimi issoku movement, entering into the side of uke with a single step.

3 Looking in the same direction as uke, tori turns by pivoting on his left foot, turning uke with him and destroying his balance.

4 Tori takes uke's collar and, by reversing his body weight, turns to face in the opposite direction. This involves the tenkai ashi movement, a 180-degree pivot on the balls of both feet, transferring the body weight from a frontal direction to behind.

5 Tori, stepping in with his rear foot, cuts down across uke's neck to bring him down. The power of the throw is effected by a strong turn of the hips, plus an attitude of cutting down the centre line of your own body, rotating the arm as if sticking the thumb into the mat.

Step 2: the power of weight transfer
Tori transfers his weight from his right foot to his left in step 2 as he turns. This completely destroys uke's balance prior to the throw in steps 3 and 4.

Irimi-nage
The movement of irimi-nage is executed across uke's body. Tori enters more into the side than directly to the front as he cuts to fell uke. Tori extends his fingers and cuts down as if trying to dig his thumb into the mat.

Shikaku
In the gyaku hanmi irimi-nage ura waza sequence shown here it is important that tori enters deeply behind uke into the position known as the shikaku, or blind spot. In this position uke's back is effectively in front of tori's chest.

Shomen-uchi Shiho-nage Omote

The execution of this front-head-strike four-direction throw technique is the same as for ai hanmi katate-dori shiho-nage (see page 70). The difference is the attack, so once tori has parried the initial strike and extended uke's arm, the concluding movements are the same.

1 Uke prepares to step forward and make a strike at tori with shomen-uchi (a front head strike).

2 Tori extends her right sword arm, harmonizing with the blow. Stepping off the central line of the attack, she uses both hands to grip uke's wrist.

3 Tori diverts uke's energy with a turn of her hips. At this point uke cannot generate any power in his arm and is thus powerless to resist tori's technique.

4 Tori follows up the manoeuvre by stepping in with her rear foot, stepping under uke's arm, and pivoting 180 degrees.

5 Tori cuts down with her whole body causing uke to fall backwards. Tori does this by imagining uke's elbow as the tip of a sword and his wrist as the handle of that sword and then cuts as if she is cutting from her centre of gravity.

Shomen-uchi Irimi-nage Ura

The difference between this front-head strike technique and ai hanmi katate-dori irimi-nage is only the attack. Shomen-uchi is a strike, katate-dori is a grab. After the strike has been parried (see below), the actual body movements of the two techniques are the same.

1 In this sequence, uke prepares to launch a strike with shomen-uchi.

2 Tori "blends" with the attack by entering forward and deflecting the blow with her raised sword arm.

3 Tori enters deeply behind uke, cutting his arm down and breaking his balance, making him start to fall backwards. In this position tori has grabbed uke's collar from behind with her left hand, and is pulling backwards and controlling his right arm with her right handblade.

4 Pivoting on her left foot, tori draws uke's energy out in a circular fashion, causing him to lose his balance.

5 By transferring her body weight from one foot to the other, tori is able to cut down across uke's neck with her arm, gaining full control.

6 Finally, tori steps in with her rear foot to bring about a throw.

Yokomen-uchi Udekime-nage Ura

This side-head strike technique involves crossed arms and a throw from behind uke. This shows the control of yokomen-uchi by entering rapidly and dominating before the attack has generated any power. Tori's left-hand contact is a parry deflecting uke's power backwards and downwards.

1 Uke prepares to launch a strike with yokomen-uchi, or a side-head strike. There are three ways in which this attack can be dealt with: stepping underneath it; stepping inside it circularly; or entering and dominating.

2 Tori enters with tsugi ashi and cuts down on the attacking arm before it can generate power. This is basically a follow-up step whereby the forward foot enters sliding on the balls of the feet and the back foot "follows up" behind it. The idea is to overwhelm an attack at the moment it starts.

3 Cutting down with her left hand and gripping uke's wrist, tori makes tenkan and extends her left arm under uke's elbow.

4 Tori drives her left hip forward and levers uke's elbow, causing him to roll forward to escape the pressure.

Shomen-uchi Kokyu-nage

A kokyu-nage, or breath throw, is usually a formless movement practised to understand timing, coordination, ma-ai (combative distance), extension and correct breathing. There are many types and styles and they can be executed against any attack.

1 In this exercise, uke attacks tori with shomen-uchi (a frontal head strike). Tori must be ready to move forward rapidly to dominate the attack as the arm raises.

2 Uke makes shomen-uchi. Tori enters slightly with tsugi ashi using the leading foot and cuts upwards with her sword arm, deflecting uke's energy. Tori enters with ayumi ashi using the rear foot, a movement similar to normal walking.

3–4 Tori continues to step in with her rear foot. From this position, she cuts upward and then downward rapidly with her left arm inside uke's elbow, while simultaneously striking uke's midsection with her palm hand, thus sending uke into a forward flip ukemi (see also step 4 to right).

Throwing technique
In step 3, it is important to enter close in to your partner, using your body motion, not your arms, to produce the throw.

Gyaku Hanmi Katate-dori Ikkyo Omote

Ikkyo is a key technique in aikido. Subsequent techniques such as nikkyo, sankyo and yonkyo depend heavily on understanding the movements of ikkyo. This movement is a basic arm pin using a reverse-stance one-hand grab with the arm pin at the front.

1 In this sequence, uke attacks tori by gripping her in gyaku hanmi katate-dori, or reverse-stance one-hand grab.

2 Tori steps sidewards, drawing uke's balance with her, and cuts down with her left hand on his arm. This takes the power from his grip. Tori also grips uke's wrist with her left hand.

3 Tori extends both of her hands, changing her grip to control uke's elbow and wrist, while pushing with her hip across uke's line of balance.

4 Tori enters with a strong hip turn towards uke's armpit with her rear foot in a powerful movement designed to propel uke away from her.

5 Dropping her centre on uke's arm, tori causes uke to fall to the mat on his chest. Instead of relying on muscular power, this result is achieved by tori manipulating uke's arm in front of her and then extending her arms so that she can drop her body weight.

Cut back to centre
In this detail of step 2 tori is cutting back towards her centre with both hands, as if cutting with a sword. The leading handblade is more positive than the rear one – this ensures that uke's power is taken away and his balance is destroyed. As a result of this uke cannot generate any power in his grip and is therefore rendered vulnerable to the technique that follows.

Ai Hanmi Katate-dori Nikkyo Ura

In this mutual-stance one-handed grab, tori's handblade rolls across the forearm. Nikkyo is a powerful technique that can be painful if uke does not take ukemi properly. He should neutralize the movement by accepting the wrist torsion and pushing his forearm towards tori's body.

1 Here, uke (the person who receives the technique) launches an attack on tori (the person who delivers the technique) with katate- or kosa-dori, meaning a one hand, or crossed hand, grab.

2 Tori traps uke's hand against her wrist (see detail below) and changes her posture, cutting into his wrist with her right handblade.

3 Tori cuts down on uke's wrist using her handblade with a kind of cutting/rolling of the radius bone in uke's forearm. This forces uke to the floor.

4 Tori changes her grip to gain control of uke's elbow, and makes tenkan, a basic body turn, to bring him in front of her.

5 Tori drops her body weight onto uke's arm, taking him to the mat.

6 Tori effects an arm pin, turning her hips and forcing uke to tap the mat in submission. Tori achieves this by hugging uke's arm close to her body, capturing uke's wrist in the crook of her left elbow and restraining his elbow with her other forearm.

Hand detail

This close-up of step 2 shows how to trap the attacking hand. Tori traps uke's fingers against her forearm, therefore preventing his escape. Tori then just has to roll uke's forearm with her handblade to conclude the movement effectively.

Ai Hanmi Katate-dori Sankyo

Sankyo is a powerful wrist-twisting technique often used by police departments as a restraining movement. From the moment tori takes uke's hand he effects an inward-twisting motion against the hand and fingers, which is maintained until the end of the technique.

1 Uke grabs tori in katate-dori, or one-hand grab.

2 On contact, tori cuts upwards with his right sword arm cutting into the back of uke's wrist and, taking uke's wrist and elbow, leans his weight forward to unbalance uke.

3 Tori steps forward, taking uke's wrist and elbow (see detail bottom far left).

4 Keeping pressure on uke's elbow, tori manipulates uke's grip on his hand (see detail bottom middle).

5 Keeping everything else the same, tori changes hands, maintaining the twisting pressure on uke's wrist.

6 Tori steps around uke's arm, taking the back of her elbow. The combination of pressure and circular motion disorients uke.

7 Dropping his weight onto uke's arm, tori takes her to the mat (see detail below right).

8 Tori applies an immobilizing pin. He changes the hand that grips uke's, keeps the wrist twist and uses his other arm to hug uke's at the elbow.

Step 3 detail
Tori's body weight is extended onto uke's elbow. The right-hand fingers are extended backwards to loosen the grip.

Step 4 detail
Tori, having detached uke's grip, takes uke's hand and fingers and twists them inwards as he maintains left-hand contact.

Step 7 detail
Tori has changed hands but keeps the same pressure on and drops his body weight onto the back of uke's elbow.

Kata-dori Nikkyo Ura Waza

This shoulder-grab attack is more practical, involving uke grabbing tori's shoulder with one hand and potentially striking with the other. The first priority, therefore, is for tori to move off the line of attack and stretch uke sideways to unbalance him (kuzushi).

1 Uke grabs the clothing at the point of tori's shoulder.

2 Tori extends the gripped arm sideways and uses his left handblade to cut down onto uke's elbow, drawing him off balance.

3 Taking uke's wrist with both hands, tori changes his posture and, placing uke's thumb on his collar bone, then cuts down with his whole body targeting the wrist. This causes uke to fall to the mat.

4 Tori follows through, dropping his body weight onto uke's elbow.

5 Tori arrests uke's shoulder by gripping it with both his knees. He controls uke's arm by hugging it against his lower abdomen, making sure that the arm is bent and tori can see the palm of uke's hand.

Pinning action
This pinning action is used for nikkyo and kote-gaeshi. Both of tori's arms arrest uke's arm and hug it tightly. Both of tori's arms are positioned with the palms upwards. Tori tries to grip uke's wrist with the crook of his own elbow.

Yokomen-uchi Ikkyo Omote

This strike to the side of the head combined with an arm pin is a practical attack and can be likened to a strike with an implement or a punch to the side of the face. Uke attacks with his handblade and tori's objective is to control the attack before any power can be generated.

1 Uke prepares to launch an attack on tori with yokomen-uchi (see page 61).

2 To counter this attack, tori enters with tsugi ashi, which is a gliding follow-up step, extending her leading arm and cutting down with her handblade on uke before too much power can be generated.

3 Sweeping her right hand over her left, tori cuts uke's arm away in a circular motion and takes uke's arm and wrist with both of her hands.

4 Entering strongly towards uke's armpit with her left foot, tori thrusts him away with her hip and takes uke down to the floor.

5 Tori pins uke's arm, extending energy to her handblades from her tanden, or her centre of gravity. This is achieved by tori placing her left knee against uke's ribs and her right knee by his pinned wrist. Tori then pins uke's arm above the elbow and at the wrist.

Chudan Tsuki Uchi Kaiten Sankyo

This middle-thrust inward rotary wrist twist involves punching the midsection of the body. Originally this attack was known as furizuki, an upward circular thrust which developed from a knife attack. Shown here is the karate-style punch that is practised in most dojos.

1 Uke prepares to punch chudan tsuki, a middle thrust, at tori's midsection.

2 Tori evades the thrust by entering with her rear foot around the attack, parrying with her left hand and grasping uke's attacking wrist with her right.

3 Tori cuts up into uke's elbow with her left handblade and passes underneath his arm, manipulating the grip into the sankyo wrist twist. This is achieved by tori holding the back of uke's hand with her left and twisting his fingers up towards his own armpit with her right.

4 Tori applies the wrist twist and cuts down as if treating uke's elbow as the tip of a sword.

5 Tori steps around uke's projected elbow with a large entering and turning motion called irimi tenkan and ends up by uke's head. Tori changes hands simultaneously keeping the pressure on the wrist and elbow, stepping in a circular movement behind uke. Grasping his elbow, uke is brought down onto the mat.

6 Tori immobilizes uke, swapping hands simultaneously, while maintaining the sankyo grip.

Ai Hanmi Katate-dori Kote-gaeshi

This movement, literally translated as a mutual-stance one-handed grab outward wrist turn, provides an immobilizing pin to control the wrist and elbow. It is an example of nage katame waza, or throwing and pinning technique.

1 Uke grabs tori in ai hanmi katate-dori, meaning the mutual-stance one-handed grab (see page 54).

2 Tori makes the first part of tenkan by taking uke's wrist with her left hand and disengaging her right hand by rotating it. She completes the tenkan movement and drops her weight onto his wrist (see detail below), taking his balance and continuing to move.

3 Tori switches her balance and places her hand on the back of uke's hand. As if rolling uke's fingers and hand into a ball, tori applies the kote-gaeshi wrist, in turn transferring her weight from the right foot to the left.

4 Uke falls to the floor while tori maintains the pressure on his wrist.

5 Moving around uke's head, tori applies pressure to the back of uke's elbow, with her left hand pushing his elbow towards his face, causing him to roll over.

6 Tori finally applies an immobilizing pin by hugging uke's arm close to her body ensuring that the arm is bent and that the wrist and elbow are controlled. It is advisable for tori to position herself so that her body is at 45 degrees to uke's, with her right knee close to uke's head.

Step 2 detail
This close-up detail of the second step shows how tori has disengaged her right wrist from uke's grip and gripped uke's wrist with her left hand, prior to placing her hand on the back of uke's hand to then effect the kote-gaeshi throw.

Gyaku Hanmi Katate-dori Kote-gaeshi Gyaku

In this movement, literally translated as a one-handed grab with a reverse outward wrist turn, tori combats an attack by breaking the power of uke's grip, rolling her hand and fingers inward and forcing her to submit.

1 Uke launches an attack on tori in gyaku hanmi katate-dori, or reverse-stance one-hand grab.

2 Tori enters strongly with his leading foot straight towards uke, leaning his weight into the movement while cutting upwards with his left swordhand. This breaks the power of uke's grip.

3 Tori grabs the base of uke's thumb as he steps around the front of her (see detail below).

4 As tori withdraws his left leg, he places his left hand on the back of uke's hand and cuts down on the back of uke's hand rolling uke's fingers inwards.

5 To avoid the pain, uke falls to the mat. Tori keeps the controlling pressure on the wrist the whole time.

6 Finally, tori immobilizes uke by stretching her arm and drops his body weight onto uke's elbow, causing her midsection to lift. The pressing down on uke's elbow and the pulling up of her hand causes immediate discomfort and her back arches as a reflex action. The result is rapid submission by uke.

Step 3 detail
Tori disengages uke's grip by drawing back the fingers of the gripped hand and simultaneously gripping the base of uke's thumb with his right hand.

Chudan Tsuki Kote-gaeshi

This middle-thrust movement is almost identical to that of ai hanmi katate-dori kote-gaeshi (see page 86). The difference is how tori harmonizes with uke's attack. This application, which is basically a stomach punch, is also effective against a knife (tanto) attack.

1 Uke stands ready to make a chudan tsuki, or a middle thrust, attack on tori.

2 As uke thrusts forward, tori enters by stepping forward into the blind side of uke. Deflecting the thrust with his left handblade, tori then makes tenkan by pivoting 180 degrees on his left foot and parrying the thrust.

3 Tori grips uke's wrist and continues turning, leading uke's energy and unsettling her balance (see detail bottom left).

4 At this position, tori drops his centre of gravity slightly, preparing to switch his balance. It is vital for tori to keep uke's wrist in front of his centre so that he can use the centre to control uke.

5 Tori steps back, opening his body by stepping back in the opposite direction with his left foot and transferring his weight to that foot. Tori simultaneously places his hand on the back of uke's hand (see detail below right).

6 When uke falls to the floor, tori puts his right hand on her elbow and drops his body weight. Uke rolls over onto her front, where tori immobilizes her by pinning her arm against his body and controlling the wrist and elbow (see step 6 on opposite page).

Step 3 detail
This close-up detail shows the grip that tori has on uke as he begins to lead her around his centre.

Step 5 detail
Here you can see tori gripping uke's wrist with his left hand, with his right hand placed on the back of uke's hand. As tori turns and twists the wrist outwards, uke loses her balance as she tries to compensate for the discomfort.

Kata-dori Kote-gaeshi

This one-hand shoulder grab is slightly more advanced as tori does not wait for uke to make contact with her shoulder, but deflects the attack with her right handblade before uke is able to grab her.

1 Launching an attack, uke attempts to grab tori by her shoulder.

2 Stepping back just before uke can grab, tori harmonizes with the movement and cuts down uke's hand with her right handblade before contact is made. This is a deflection of uke's power.

3 Tori grips uke's wrist with her left hand and draws uke's energy forwards, causing him to lose his balance.

4 Tori places her hand on the back of uke's hand and applies kote-gaeshi by twisting his wrist outwards, as if rolling uke's fingers and hand into a ball. The pressure needs to be constant, not allowing uke to straighten his wrist and generate any power to resist.

5 Stepping around the top of uke, tori applies pressure to the back of his elbow, causing him to roll over.

6 Tori immobilizes uke's arm. As long as uke's arm is bent against tori's body and the wrist is gripped by tori's elbow, uke will be unable to resist and will submit.

Ushiro Ryote-dori Ikkyo Omote

This rear two-handed grab and arm pin is one of the ushirowaza techniques. Tori must have good balance so as not to be easily pulled backwards. Mentally tori projects uke forwards as she steps backwards. This is the basic tenet for all ushiro techniques.

1 Approaching her from the rear, uke grabs and holds both of tori's wrists – uke must ensure that he establishes a good grip on her wrists.

2 Stepping back with her leading foot, tori extends strongly forwards with both arms. Uke loses his balance forwards, a position required prior to the execution of most ushirowaza.

3 Tori straightens up and grips uke's wrist and elbow as shown. At this stage tori is preparing to enter with a gutsy thrust of her right hip as she steps in, which will send uke forwards and sideways and completely destroy his balance.

4 Taking a step forward, tori drops her body weight onto uke's arm, causing him to fall. Finally she pins his arm with extended power from her centre. There is no tension in the shoulders. Tori aims to pin uke's arm slightly higher than 90 degrees to his body.

Ikkyo arm pin
This two-handed arm pin involves pinning the arm at a position greater than 90 degrees to uke's body, higher than the shoulder. The grip has a slight push and twist. Tori imagines that the power comes from her centre of gravity.

Ushiro Ryokata-dori Sankyo Ura

Using the same principle as ushiro ryote-dori ikkyo omote, tori extends – her wrists are not gripped, but the movement is the same. Tori does not try to wrest the grip, but pushes it against her shoulder so that the shoulder's power effects the wrist-twisting motion.

1 Approaching from the rear, uke grips tori by both shoulders.

2 Tori immediately steps forward with her rear foot, simultaneously extending both of her arms to unsettle uke's balance and bring him forward.

3 Stepping back with her right foot, tori holds uke's wrist as if it were a sword. Turning her gripped shoulder inward powered by an inward hip turn, power is generated onto uke's wrist. Tori takes uke's wrist in a wringing motion with her right hand, and with her left hand applies her body weight just above uke's elbow. This wrist twist causes uke to release his grip.

4 Tori steps in a circular fashion behind uke and grips his elbow, then drops her body weight onto his arm (see also detail to right).

5 With uke now on the mat, tori immobilizes his arm, maintaining the wrist twist.

Step 4 detail
In this close-up you can see the detail of the grip just prior to tori dropping her body weight onto uke's arm.

Ushiro Katate-dori Kube-shime Kokyu-nage

In this rear one-handed grab and choke-breath throw uke grips one of tori's wrists and steps behind to apply a choke with the other arm. He grips tori's collar high up and applies pressure against the carotid artery with the collar. Tori leads uke before his grip consolidates.

1 Approaching from the front, uke grabs tori's wrist and steps behind her in an attempt to apply a choke hold.

2 Tori harmonizes with the movement, turning and extending the gripped hand over her head. She does this, not by opposing uke's power, but by leading it as she extends uke's arm over her head, continuing in one circular motion with the intent of wrapping uke's arm across his other one.

3 Tori now grasps uke's upper right sleeve and extends her left hand across her body to completely take his balance.

4 Tori now drops onto her left her knee and extends forward, projecting uke to the mat.

Ushiro Katate-dori Kube-shime Koshi-nage

The defence for this one-handed hip throw comes from koshi-nage, or a hip/waist throw, where uke's body is loaded onto tori's hips and then flipped over. The attitude for tori is not to lift uke's body, but to extend and lead his energy and present her hips for him to ride over.

1 Approaching from the front, uke grabs tori's wrist and steps behind her in an attempt to apply a choke hold.

2 Tori turns, harmonizing with uke's energy, and extends her gripped hand over her head.

3 By extending her right arm underneath uke's, tori is able to neutralize her attacker's power.

4 Now, by bending her knees and lowering her centre of gravity, uke effectively rides over tori's hips.

5 Uke flips over tori's hips and lands on the mat. Tori is not gripping uke at this stage. However, depending on how well uke has been led, there may be a need to grip uke's right elbow (as shown here) to ensure he flips over naturally and does not hurtle head first onto the mat.

Futaridori Kokyu-ho

This technique, involving tori and two ukes, is a good way of testing your kokyu-ryoku, or breath power. With one attacker holding each wrist, you need to manipulate the attackers in such a way as to be able to use your tanden and hips to drive the cutting motions of the hands.

1 In this encounter, tori's wrists are held by two ukes. The ukes are there to help tori train his breath power and not necessarily to struggle against everything that tori does.

2 Tori, using a strong hip-turning motion, steps forward and cuts upwards with his left sword arm as if raising a sword.

3 Withdrawing his right foot in a circular movement backwards, as if drawing a bowstring, tori takes his right arm back and cuts across both of his partners with his left sword arm. It is important to keep both ukes close together.

4 Tori draws his partners underneath his left arm, stretching them both fully and compromising their balance. This is achieved using circular movement and extension of ki.

5 Finally, tori leans his centre of gravity forwards and fells them both.

Futaridori Nikkyo

This is a defence technique against two attackers holding both of tori's wrists. It relies on a rapid and forceful step forward to draw the attackers forward, and then another step quickly backwards so that they do not have time to regain their posture.

1 Tori's wrists are held by two attackers. Tori extends both arms, imagining ki is flowing through his fingers.

2 Stepping quickly forward with his rear foot, tori leans his body weight forward to draw his partners in front of him.

3 Drawing his elbows together, tori cuts upwards from his centre of gravity. He does this with his two sword arms close together, driven by a strong hip lift, in a similar movement to the way a weightlifter would get his body underneath a weight. This has the effect of bringing the two partners together.

4 Tori simultaneously extends both hands over the top of his partners' wrists without actually grabbing them. Tori's shoulders must be relaxed and his attitude one of cutting over the top of both ukes' wrists.

5 With a type of cutting roll of both of ukes' radius bones in the forearm, tori exerts a painful impulse with his two handblades, forcing his partners' forearms down. Don't try to force the ukes' forearms down with direct pressure on the wrists – this will never work. The movement has a rotating cut which is difficult for the ukes to resist, so they are forced to harmonize with the movement.

Weapons and Advanced Training

This chapter includes a brief overview of weapons training from the many approaches that are available. Subjects covered include how to hold weapons and the postures and attitudes to use; how to use weapons with examples of basic cuts and thrusts with the bokken (wooden sword) and jo (wooden staff); basic partner practices such as uchi komi, awase or blending exercises; and disarming a knife-wielding aggressor, or tanto dori. The chapter also looks at kicking techniques, or geri waza, which are suitable for more advanced students because of the danger of injury, and self-defence techniques, also an advanced training method because classic aikido movements need careful adaptation to suit the requirements of contemporary self-defence.

Handling and Using Weapons

The first thing you learn with weapons is how to hold them. You have to hold the bokken and jo strongly with the little finger and the next finger up of each hand. The middle and forefingers hold in a loose manner. This grip permits rapid manoeuvrability and the ability to parry and strike quickly. It approximates to the same grip you have on the steering wheel of a car when driving or when you hold a knife and fork.

The tsuka, or handle, of the bokken is held with the left hand and with the little finger parallel to the bottom. The right hand should be about three-widths of a finger up from the left hand, so that the forefinger can just touch the tsuba, or the protective handguard. The grip on the jo is the same as with the bokken, but you need to spread your hands wider apart.

One of the biggest problems you will encounter is how to generate the necessary power for the sword to cut properly. The rule is that "the sword cuts, not you". Even though the bokken is wooden, you have to treat it as if it were a live blade – otherwise the whole concept of sword training loses reality. The cut with a live Japanese blade always occurs on the backstroke, so you have to project the blade over the top of the intended target and then allow the speed and gravity of the weapon to slice through it effortlessly.

LEARNING THE BOKKEN, OR BOKUTO
The traditional division of weapon techniques can be classified as follows:
- **Suburi:** Solo exercises designed to help you understand how to hold the sword, how to do basic cuts and thrusts, how to change direction and maintain your balance and how to harmonize body and weapon so that they feel as one.
- **Uchikomi:** Encountering a partner for the first time. You learn five sets of movements that allow you and your partner to practise timing, coordination and the concept of ma-ai, combative distance awareness. You are also introduced to the idea of avoiding the central line of attack. The practice involves moving up and down the dojo with a partner cutting and thrusting in different combinations.
- **Awase:** A blending exercise. Here you and your partner remain in one place and practise simple one- or two-step cutting and thrusting movements.
- **Kumitachi:** In this more advanced partner training, movements become more complex and contain variations that go some way to bridging the gap

between weapon training and body art (tai jutsu). Some of these advanced techniques involve throws and joint locks and promote the concept of riai, which means "blending of truths". At this level of training, one learns to move as if weapons are an integral part, or extensions of the body.
- **Tachidori:** This is the highest level of weapon training in which an unarmed individual learns to face a sword-wielding aggressor.

LEARNING THE JO
The sequence of learning the jo is very similar to that of the bokken.
- **Suburi** and **jo awase:** Both these terms have the same meaning as the sword (see above).
- **Kumijo:** These more elaborate movements are practised for the same reasons as for the bokken.
- **Jo kata:** Continuous cutting, thrusting and striking movements that are performed solo with the jo. These can be performed only once the basics of suburi are fully understood.
- **Jo dori:** Again, the highest level of training within aiki jo whereby an attacker thrusts and is disarmed with a variety of throwing and pinning techniques.

Weapon terminology
Throughout this chapter you will come across the traditional Japanese terms used to describe the names of the techniques and the names of the partners in the scenarios.

Uchitachi The partner who attacks with the bokken.

Uketachi The partner who performs the technique.

Uchijo The partner who attacks with the jo.

Ukejo The partner who performs the technique.

The Five Postures of the Bokken

These are the five basic ways of holding the bokken (wooden sword) in traditional aikido weapon training: held along the centre line, held above the head, held to the right of the head, hidden from your partner and held low.

1 The first posture is chudan no kamae, the most basic of all the postures. The bokken is held in the centre line of the body with the tip pointing toward your partner's eyes. **2** The second is jodan no kamae, where the sword is held above the head.

3 When the sword is held at the right side of the head, it is called hasso no kamae. **4** The fourth posture, wakigame no kamae is, in effect, hiding the sword. **5** When the sword is held low, as shown here, the posture is known as gedan.

The Five Postures of the Jo

These are the five basic ways of holding the jo (short staff) in traditional aikido weapon training: the basic posture, held in front as a sword, held high as a sword, held vertically, and held in readiness on the ground.

1 The basic jo posture chudan no kamae. **2** Chudan no kamae where the jo is held in front of you as a sword. **3** The third posture, where the jo is held as a sword above the head.

4 In hasso no kamae the jo is held vertically to the right side of your head. **5** In the fifth posture of readiness, the jo rests on the floor and the hand position can vary according to the context.

Weapon Attack: Shomen-uchi

When practising this front-head strike, it is good ma-ai, or combative distance awareness, to be able to take one step to reach the target. The area that cuts, called the monouchi, is on the cutting edge of the blade 4cm (1½in) from the tip to a further 20cm (8in) downwards.

1 Uchitachi, the attacking practitioner, stands in chudan no kamae opposite uketachi, the person who receives. Uchitachi extends his ki down the blade.

2 Uchitachi raises his sword as he steps back. From here uketachi has no idea whether the attack will be shomen or yokomen-uchi.

3 Stepping forward, uchitachi cuts to the centre of uketachi's head.

Weapon Attack: Yokomen-uchi

The attack movement of this side-head strike is the same as shomen-uchi (above), but the target area of the cut is directed to the side of uketachi's head. Because the sword is raised in the same wasy as shomen-uchi, it is difficult for uketachi to forsee the direction of the attack.

1 Uchitachi, or the attacking practitioner, stands in chudan no kamae opposite uketachi.

2 Uchitachi raises his sword as he steps back. From here uketachi has no idea whether the attack will be shomen- or yokomen-uchi.

3 This time the cut is directed at the side of uketachi's head.

Weapon Attack: Tsuki

This movement, meaning "thrust", is a similar attack to a punch to tori's midsection. For those familiar with the tsuki "kendo", thrust (where the body is held square on to uketachi), this thrust differs as it has uchitachi moving into hanmi, or half stance, to deliver the thrust.

1 Uchitachi stands with both his feet together, with his sword pointing at uketachi. This is a practice for uchitachi to execute tsuki in hanmi (left or right).

2 Uchitachi, sliding his front foot forward, prepares to thrust.

3 Uchitachi completes the tsuki attack by targeting the side of the neck, as shown, or uketachi's throat. Uchitachi reverts back to step 1, then makes tsuki in left hanmi.

Counter Attack: Kirigaeshi

Kirigaeshi, or countering cut, is a defensive, as opposed to offensive, cut. It is a response to an attack and involves moving off the line of a straight cut or thrust, parrying the strike and then responding with an attack yourself.

1 The partners face each other. It is essential to have an appropriate distance (ma-ai) between partners.

2 Uchitachi steps off the line of an imaginary attack, protecting his body and head with his sword.

3 Uchitachi changes posture and raises his sword. He steps off the attacking line with his left foot, bringing his right foot to his left and then stepping back with that right foot as he cuts with the sword. Uchitachi is here learning to step off the line of potential attack and deliver the counter attack.

4 Stepping back, uchitachi makes a defensive shomen-uchi (front-head strike).

Renzoku Uchikomi: Shomen Uchikomi

The movements of renzoku uchikomi, continuous stepping and striking practice, are traditional partner exercises practised up and down the dojo in left and right hanmi. Usually there are five renzoku uchikomi, of which the first three are shown here.

1 Chudan no kamae is the basic posture of partner sword practice. It is also called seigan, and is employed when both partners' weapons touch about 5–7.5cm (2–3in) from their tips, and while the tips point at each other's eyes.

2 Uchitachi steps forward and raises her sword to cut with shomen-uchi. Uketachi extends his sword towards the attacking sword to meet it and steps backwards in a circular manner.

3 Uketachi draws his sword down to the centre of his body, neutralizing the attack. This continues as uchitachi in step 2 steps forward onto her left leg and strikes again. Uketachi repeats, but this time in left hanmi. This continues up and down the dojo.

Renzoku Uchikomi: Tsuki Uchikomi

This movement is a basic attack-and-defence scenario involving tsuki uchikomi (continuous thrusting and stepping). The body moves in the same way as the previous technique, and as above it involves parrying rather than blocking or trying to stop the movement.

1 This exercise starts in the seigan posture. Uketachi extends his sword across uchitachi's weapon in an attempt to lead her into an attack. Uchitachi maintains contact with uketachi's sword until it passes across her centre line, when uketachi can no longer control it.

2 As her blade is now not under control, uchitachi is free to attack. She steps forward with her left foot coming up underneath uketachi's parry and makes the tsuki attack, stepping off the line.

3 Uketachi steps circularly back with his right foot, cutting up the centre line of his body and deflects the thrust. Uketachi leads uchitachi's blade as in step 1, but from the opposite side, enabling continuous practice up and down the dojo.

Renzoku Uchikomi: Kirigaeshi Uchikomi

This is the basic way to practise kirigaeshi, a countering technique with a partner using the same body movement as the previous techniques. This enables the practice of musubi or tying together, where partners try to maintain weapon contact for as long as possible.

1 Uchitachi and uketachi face each other in seigan. This is also known as chudan no kamae, or middle posture and is the start position for all aikiken practice.

2 Uketachi presses down on uchitachi's blade with his own. This is a way to lead your partner into a practice. Originally, in a real combat situation, this movement would have been used to knock down uketachi's blade prior to launching a direct attack.

3 Uchitachi maintains the contact between the weapons and steps beneath and to the side of uketachi's blade, parrying, protecting and cutting in a single movement called kirigaeshi.

4 Uchitachi raises her sword to make a counter attack.

5 Uchitachi makes a left-foot shomen-uchi, meaning a strike to the front of uketachi's head.

6 Uketachi steps back circularly, drawing his sword back to his body's centre line and parrying the strike. This final position illustrates how, by moving off the attacking centre line, it is possible to deflect an attack enough to eliminate danger.

Jo Awasewaza: Makiotoshi Against Shomen-uchi

This jo awasewaza (staff blending) movement called makiotoshi (twisting down movement) is a powerful defence. It aims to propel uchijo's weapon back towards him and to strike his leading hand. Ukejo should visualize dropping her centre of gravity down her partner's centreline.

1 Ukejo, the partner who performs the technique, and uchijo, the partner who attacks with the jo, initially face each other in ai hanmi, both holding the jo in gyakute, or reverse hand.

2 Uchijo makes shomen-uchi, or a front-head strike with the jo, raising it up his left side to an above-head position.

3 Ukejo moves slightly to the side raising her jo to parry the attack.

4 Ukejo propels the attacking jo away by rolling her jo down her partner's jo with a wrist action, while leaning her body weight into the action to cut the thumb or fingers of the attacker. Uchijo's attitude should be to neutralize this action by letting go with the target hand and then allowing the weapon to flow backwards.

Jo Awasewaza: Makiuchiotoshi Against Tsuki

This second jo awasewaza movement is called makiuchiotoshi (twisting-down striking drop). While the intent is clearly martial, safe practice requires the targeting of an area on the jo as near to the hand as possible to avoid causing injury.

1 As uchijo prepares to thrust at ukejo, ukejo steps slightly off the attacking line. Turning her body, she revolves the jo, parrying the thrust, using the left hand as a fulcrum.

2 Ukejo continues to make a large, circular strike against uchijo's leading hand. The idea is to strike the hand and the weapon down – uchijo is aware of this and lets go before impact.

3 As uchijo's attack nears its target and she drops her weight onto the attacking weapon, uchijo lets go with his leading hand and allows the impact to drive his jo downwards.

Jo Awasewaza: Junteuchiotoshi Against Kesa Giri

Junteuchiotoshi (front hand-striking drop) involves turning the upper body and meeting the attacking jo, but not blocking it. Kesa giri is a diagonal strike to the side of the head/neck that follows the angle of the gi jacket as it is wrapped around from the left shoulder to the right hip.

1 Uchijo and ukejo face each other in ai hanmi. Note the different ways that both partners are holding the jo.

2 Uchijo raises his jo to make kesa giri (a diagonal cut) – the target being the side of the head or neck.

3 Ukejo raises her jo to meet the attack, turning her body to face it and parries the strike. The impact of an attack like this can be great. Ukejo's grip on the jo must be strong enough not to allow the weapon to give way, but resilient enough not to generate stiffness.

4 With a feeling of dropping her body weight and rolling the jo down that of the attacking weapon...

5 ...ukejo makes a large circular movement, protecting herself and propelling the attacking weapon away. Her attitude is to strike uchijo's leading hand in the process. He, in turn, must adopt an attitude of neutralizing the attack by harmonizing with it, so he lets go of the weapon with the targeted hand.

6 From above her head, ukejo makes a tsuki thrust in one movement. She does this, having knocked down the attacking jo, by thrusting her own weapon towards uchijo's midsection causing him to bend backwards to avoid it. Ukejo's whole body is behind this thrust, making it a formidable strike.

Tanto Dori: Tsuki Kote-gaeshi

Tanto dori is a knife defence and must be taken very seriously. Although wooden weapons are used, the tanto has to be handled as if it were a live blade where the slightest touch of the blade would cut. Tori's prime directive is to wrest the tanto from uke.

1 Uke prepares to thrust at tori's midsection using a chudan tsuki, or middle thrust.

2 As uke thrusts, tori enters around the attack using irimi ashi (see page 49), stepping in with his rear foot, and parrying before then gripping uke's wrist (tori must parry first).

3 Tori makes tenkan, pivoting on his leading foot by 180 degrees, and drops his weight on the captured wrist.

4 Stepping back with his right foot behind uke and transferring his weight forward, tori places his hand on the back of uke's and makes kote-gaeshi, turning uke's wrist and arm outwards and downwards, causing them to buckle and uke to fall to the mat.

5 As uke falls to the mat tori pins her arm, making sure that the tanto is taken away as soon as possible.

Tanto Dori: Tsuki Katagatame

Another tanto dori, or knife-defence action the success of this technique relies on controlling the weapon quickly and hugging the arm against the body, controlling uke's wrist and elbow and keeping the blade facing away.

1 Standing in ai hanmi, or mutual stance, tori prepares for uke's thrust with the tanto. Tori must be alert and ready, as at this stage it is difficult to determine what attack is coming.

2 Tori turns his body (kaiten) and deflects the attack. Kaiten is a rotating movement of the hips, pivoting on the balls of the feet so that you are facing the same direction as the attack. Tori uses his right handblade to deflect the attacking arm.

3 Tori cuts down with his right hand and arrests uke's knife-wielding arm with both of his arms. Once the tanto is controlled, tori drops his centre of gravity. As long as uke's arm is bent against tori's body she will be unable to generate any power.

4 This movement causes uke to drop to the mat.

5 Tori immobilizes uke's arm by hugging the arm close to the body and turning his right shoulder towards uke's head. This creates strong pressure on the shoulder and forces uke to submit or risk a potential dislocation of the shoulder. At this point tori takes away the tanto, ensuring that it is safely out of the way.

Tanto Dori: Yokomen-uchi Gokkyo

This knife-defence action is carried out in combination with a side-head strike and arm stretch. The attack here can be when the tanto is held as if to stab like a dagger or to slash like a small sword.

1 Uke prepares to launch a strike at the side of tori's head or neck using yokomen-uchi, or a side-head strike.

2 Tori enters with ayumi ashi. He steps forward with his rear foot in a movement similar to normal walking, but moves both feet across slightly to keep out of uke's centre line. Tori then cuts down on uke's arm with his right handblade, while taking her wrist with his other hand. This grip has tori's thumb underneath uke's wrist and therefore applies forward pressure on the wrist – preventing any movement of the blade in uke's grip.

3 Having controlled the tanto, tori extends his arms in front in a large sweeping motion as he turns, controlling uke's arm. Tori then steps forward and drops his centre of gravity onto uke's arm. From here tori continues forward towards uke's armpit, taking her balance slightly sideways.

4 This movement causes uke to drop to the mat. Tori's reverse grip with the left hand, which remains the same throughout this sequence, is essential for this technique.

5 Tori stretches uke's arm outwards and then bends her wrist back, as shown. Strong pressure is then exerted on the wrist against the mat – this causes the fingers to open so that the tanto can be removed.

Tanto Dori: Yokomen-uchi Shiho-nage

This knife attack uses a side-head strike. Generally the knife is held as if it is a small sword. The secret in this sequence is to step inside the circular slashing movement and parry, rather than block, uke's movement.

1 Tori (on the left) prepares for uke's yokomen uchi with a tanto.

2 Uke makes a large circular slash at tori's head. Tori steps inside of the attack, parrying it with his left handblade.

3 Cutting down with his left hand, tori takes uke's wrist with both hands and extends in front, taking uke's balance.

4 Tori steps in with his back foot and passes under uke's arm, turning 180 degrees. At this point, tori controls uke's wrist and the tanto and begins to cut downwards causing uke to fall to the mat. The knife handle must be controlled to turn uke's wrist inwards.

5 Tori makes tenkan, pivoting 180 degrees on his right foot, while gripping uke's wrist with his right hand. With a cutting-down motion tori wrests the tanto from uke's grip with his left hand, pinning her wrist to the mat (see detail below).

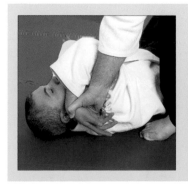

Step 5 detail
This detail shows the final pin on uke's wrist after the tanto has been taken away. Tori bears his weight onto the wrist and pushes slightly inwards to ensure there is no gap between uke's wrist and her head. This immobilizes uke.

Kicking Techniques

Kicking techniques, or geri waza, represent more advanced aikido training, and they can be dangerous if not practised properly. Because nearly all require a fluent understanding of ushiro ukemi, or backward breakfall (see page 57), they are often omitted from training. Some factions of aikido do not recognize geri waza as orthodox, although the exercises that follow were taught by a uchideshi, or live-in student, of aikido founder, Morihei Ueshiba.

Kicking techniques represent a fascinating insight into the practical applications of aikido. In any study of traditional aikido, you cannot understand how it has evolved if you do not go back to its roots. If the martial heritage of aikido is ignored then it ceases to be a budo, or martial way, and becomes nothing more than an elaborate system of exercise.

By their very nature kicking techniques are martial. Practice therefore must be conducted in a positive but controlled manner. Kicking is a very real threat in today's society, but by applying the core principles of aikido body movement, kicking attacks can be easily controlled.

The following techniques are three variations on irimi-nage, or an entering throw. There are many more defences against kicks that cannot be included. The examples here involve defences against maegeri, or a front kick. There are also defences against other kicking attacks, such as mawashi-geri, or a roundhouse kick, but in an introduction to aikido such as this they are not covered.

Chudan Maegeri Irimi-nage – Variation 1

The kicking area used in chudan maegeri, or middle front kick, is the ball of the foot. The knee is lifted in front of the body and then the lower leg is launched from that position. In aikido you never try to block such an attack, but always to parry or deflect it.

1 Tori faces uke in gyaku hanmi, or reverse stance.

2 Uke strikes with chudan maegeri by lifting the knee in front of the body and then kicking the lower leg. Tori deflects the kick with his right hand as he makes irimi issoku, or one-step entering.

3 Entering deeply with his left foot as he parries the kick to uke's side, tori places his right hand under uke's leg and extends his left hand across uke's front to dominate any strike from his right hand, and to cut across his neck. With his leg in the air and leaning back as a result of the dominance of tori's hand movement, uke is totally off balance.

4 Tori extends his body weight forward to bring uke down to the mat.

Chudan Maegeri Irimi-nage – Variation 2

This is another variation of the chudan maegeri, or middle front kick. The movements below could be just as easily applied to a front strike to the head (shomen-uchi) or a punch to the face or stomach (chudan-/jodan-tsuki).

1 Tori and uke face each other in ai hanmi, and uke prepares to strike tori's midsection with a front kick.

2 As uke steps and kicks with his right leg, tori deflects the attack and enters with his back foot with ayumi ashi, in a slightly exaggerated walking movement that also moves off the line of attack. Tori avoids blocking the kick, which would result in a broken forearm.

3 Continuing the entering momentum, tori cuts across uke's neck, causing him to lose balance, or kuzushi. With a feeling of dropping his centre of gravity, tori can then bring uke to the mat.

4 Tori has executed irimi-nage in the same way as he would from any other attack – avoiding the central line of attack, then entering and throwing.

Chudan Maegeri Irimi-nage Ura

This is the third way of executing the principle of irimi-nage, or entering throw. The first two techniques are examples of omote, or movements directly to the front of uke. This is an example of ura, where completion takes place behind uke.

1 Tori and uke confront each other in gyaku hanmi, or opposite stance.

2 Uke kicks and tori parries uke's kick sideways, therefore avoiding its force. He then steps in deeply with his front foot and then onto his left foot to get behind uke.

3 Tori takes uke's shoulders. If this is done while the kick is still happening, the combination of pulling him backwards and downwards makes it easy to fell uke. Tori is in the classic shikaku or blind-spot position, where it is difficult for uke to retain his balance, or to launch any kind of counter-attack.

4 Tori drops his body weight onto uke's shoulders while pulling back and pushing down. This causes uke to lose his balance, after which tori is able to bring him down.

Aikido and Self-defence

When considering taking up aikido, ask yourself what you expect. It is a traditional art, one that incorporates training against the weapons already described, as well as nearly every type of unarmed attack. The founder also wove his religious and philosophical beliefs into aikido, giving it spiritual aspects that have become a magnet to those not necessarily interested in pure combat, but also to those who want something they can apply in their daily lives.

Many people cite self-defence as the main reason for beginning aikido, so it is the responsibility of instructors to make sure that prospective candidates are aware of what self-defence means in the context of the art.

A PRAGMATIC AND CO-OPERATIVE ART

In the early 1970s, Chiba Sensei, the technical director for the Aikikai of Great Britain and the official delegate from the Hombu in Japan, was asked about aikido and self-defence: "How, if aikido is an art that teaches us to harmonize with an attack, can victory be secured against several people coming at you if all you do is harmonize with them and you don't try to hurt them?" Sensei's answer was: "You are thinking too much in terms of the religious side of the art. Aikido is a martial way that recognizes individuals' rights to defend themselves, and to do what is necessary to control a situation."

If we look back to the days of the samurai in feudal Japan we see that the martial arts they practised had to be effective on the battlefield. Society was governed then by military

Below The final stage of hanmi handachi shiho-nage where tori approaches the kneeling uke from behind. Here, uke bends with the movement prior to taking ukemi.

warlords who employed samurai warriors as retainers, and these warlords had to find ways to train their samurais to be unbeatable. Thus, a huge number of martial ryu, or schools, sprang up. If the warriors in your service were the best trained, then you won and accrued land, property and wealth.

When you begin your training it should be made clear to you that most of the regular practice in the dojo is what is called "conditioning training". It is geared towards conditioning the body in terms of understanding the mechanics of the techniques and in physical training – conditioning the mind in terms of understanding kokyu and ki (see pages 27–31) – very little training in actual self-defence movements takes place. The thinking behind this is that you are conditioning your body in preparation for the martial art, not in the martial art itself. So you should not be surprised to find that practice is conducted in a spirit of co-operation between partners, and that you never try to compete with or resist your partner during practice. This is in line with the founder's philosophy of harmony and non-violence and reflects the fact that aikido movements are the same movements that are seen in nature.

DIVERSITY

Aikido is taught traditionally through the dissemination of core principles from which all of the movements and techniques stem, rather than by showing masses of techniques, and it is this commonality that, paradoxically, enables the art to be interpreted in many ways. It is fascinating to note that the world's greatest aikido masters, men who have sat at the feet of aikido's founder, Morihei Ueshiba, through differences in build, temperament and motivation came away with, in some cases, unique ideas on aikido and went on to develop their own styles of the art. This is one reason why different people are attracted to different shihan, or master teachers. Regarding weapons, some advocate that it is not necessary to train with them at all, while others follow the classical weapons style of the late grandmaster Saito Shihan. There are several prominent shihan who have gone on to create entirely new weapon systems and styles that incorporate elements of other martial arts the shihan have studied. It is likely that Ueshiba would have been happy with these differences in interpretation

Above Ukemi, the art of falling or recovery, is vital in developing the confidence to neutralize the effect of a throw. Students need to learn to fall both forwards and backwards, the latter shown here.

Above Kung-fu master Bruce Lee introduced the martial arts into popular Hollywood culture. Here, he executes a mawashi-geri, or roundhouse kick, in his film *Fist of Fury* (1972).

of his art. He is said to have stated on his deathbed that "Aikido is for the World", and that he had only scratched the surface of what was on offer.

LEARNING THE ART

When beginners enrol at a dojo, they will be taught how to roll forwards and backwards and how to do taisabaki, or body movements. Next they will begin partner practices that lead to kihon waza, or basic technique. This training teaches you how to harmonize with an attack, redirect it and then apply a technique to neutralize it. When receiving the technique, you will first attack your partner with full commitment. Then, as the technique is applied, you will neutralize its effect by blending with it rather than trying to escape from it. As you progress to more advanced training, the movements become more sophisticated – but it is essentially the same as that encountered in basic training.

When you tell people that 90 per cent of aikido is conditioning training, in which you train with a co-operative partner, many draw the conclusion that the art is impracticable. Even 30 years of slow-motion training in wrist-grabbing techniques will not prepare you for a street mugger. You have to train for the situations you think you might have to deal with. Aikido is as good, if not better, than most martial arts for self-defence, but you have to change the training criteria in order to be successful. Techniques against a punch, for example, have to be modified, as there was no concept of this in the original art. The attack we know today as chudan tsuki (see page 61) was originally called furizuki, which is an upward circular thrust with a knife, so we have to take account of this and modify the training where necessary.

You have to ask yourself if you are ever likely to be assaulted with a sword, spear or halberd. The answer is likely to be "No". A street fighter will have no understanding of

harmony, musubi, contact or ukemi. He will try to resist anything you attempt and will not necessarily make a "committed attack", preferring to adjust his balance as and when, much as a boxer would. Cross-training with other martial arts is a must if self-defence is your priority. If you want to use aikido to defend yourself against a boxer, then train with a boxer – but one you know! If you want to defend yourself against a street attack, train with a street fighter. You have to become familiar with the situation that you are training for, and you must do that by experiencing the situation in a controlled environment with somebody who will point out the problems with your defence strategies.

In this scenario it is fairly certain that aikido is sufficiently resilient to contain any situation. Any quality martial art will give exponents an advantage over an untrained attacker – with physical fitness, mental and spiritual training, stamina, co-ordination and timing providing that all-important edge. Public perception of martial arts is a major contributory factor in their credibility. Over the years, Hollywood films, and the media in general, have not done martial arts any favours. The notion of one man taking on and defeating 20 armed villains has done precious little for local dojo instructors trying to recruit members, as the public perception is that the martial arts are only for the lunatic fringe, for people who think they can run up walls and fly through the treetops.

Anybody looking for self-defence techniques must be aware that it is necessary to train realistically to be successful in real situations, so expect the odd bloody nose or black eye in the dojo. Many people expect too much for too little effort: they join a dojo and if they cannot fight like Bruce Lee in two weeks they throw in the towel. Committed individuals need to find an experienced instructor who understands their self-defence needs, and who will work with them to devise extra-curricular training to concentrate on achieving their goals.

Self-defence Techniques

The following sequences show scenarios where aikido techniques have been modified to suit particular situations where self-defence is required, such as defending yourself from a bag snatcher, or a punch to the face. It is essential that a student must have a thorough knowledge of the techniques that these movements are based on in order to adapt them successfully and carry them out in a non-controlled environment.

All these techniques come under the category of oyowaza, or applied techniques, and, as the name suggests, are practical applications where the intent is to enable an escape from a potentially serious situation. In each case their application would be short and sharp and with no consideration for uke (as there would be in general practice). These movements have been chosen because they are relatively simple and quick to apply and because it is easy to see at a glance which techniques they are derived from. As a general rule simple manoeuvres are better in a self-defence situation.

Defending a Head Attack from Behind

This sequence, the first example of oyowaza, is an application of nikkyo and shows a method of defending a hair-grabbing attack from behind. The mechanics of nikkyo, or wrist in turn, need to be understood before this technique can work.

1 In this attack from behind, uke grabs tori's hair.

2 Tori traps uke's hand with interlocked fingers (see detail below) and pushes his hand against her head while turning to face uke.

3 Drawing her leg back sharply, tori cuts into the back of uke's wrist by turning her head down and inwards. It is quite possible, at this point, that the sudden pressure on the wrist would cause the assailant to let go immediately. In this case tori could get away without necessarily having to hit uke with her knee.

4 The pressure on the wrist brings uke's head down and forward, enabling tori to strike his face with her knee. The purpose of aikido is not to cause injury if at all possible. However, here is a situation where the youth may not let go of the girl's hair immediately, in which case the girl can bring her knee full force into the attacker's face.

Step 2 detail
This shows a close up of the interlocked fingers pushing uke's hand onto tori's head. Tori needs to cut into the back of uke's wrist sharply before he realizes what is happening.

Defence from a Bag Snatcher

This sequence, which is an application of kote-gaeshi, is an effective method of defending an attempt to snatch your bag. It involves taking control from the bag snatcher so that you are controlling him, as well as securing the bag.

1 Tori searches through her bag as she is approached by uke.

2 Uke makes a grab for the bag but tori holds on with her right hand.

3 Tori pulls with her right hand to enable her to take uke's wrist.

4 Without wresting uke's grip from the bag, tori grabs the back of uke's wrist and applies the kote-gaeshi wrist turn (see detail).

5 This pressure causes uke to fall. Tori maintains the wrist action.

6 While stepping around uke's head tori switches hands and applies strong pressure on the back of uke's elbow which, coupled with the twisting action on the wrist, causes extreme discomfort to uke (see detail).

Step 4 detail
Holding uke's right wrist with her left hand, tori places her right hand around uke's fist on the strap, as if she is embracing uke's hand. With a sharp inward squeezing and rolling action, tori breaks the power in uke's grip.

Step 6 detail
Applying strong pressure on the back of uke's elbow as well as a wrist-twisting action, tori causes extreme discomfort to uke. This, along with a few harsh words requesting the handbag's release, should be all that is needed.

Defending a Neck Grab

This sequence is a practical application of rokkyo or arm smashing. Because it is applied directly against the natural movement of the joint, if uke's arm is pinned against tori's body and an inward hip movement employed, the elbow can be broken.

1 Tori takes in a view at a park when she is approached by a stranger who realizes that she is alone. It is difficult at this stage to know what the stranger's intentions are.

2 Uke, or the stranger, attempts to grab her by the neck, so tori takes the underside of uke's wrist with her right hand.

3 Reinforcing her grip by bringing her other hand up, tori rotates uke's arm as she turns away from him.

4 Tori hugs uke's arm against her body keeping it straight and effects a powerful hip turn applying strong pressure directly against the elbow joint.

Defending a Punch to the Face

This sequence is an application of ikkyo, or the arm pin. The final pin is executed with strong pressure against the back of uke's wrist and just above the elbow to the ground. The pinning pressure comes from the tanden, or centre of gravity.

1 As uke steps forward to strike tori's face, tori parries the thrust, keeping his right hand in contact with the back of uke's wrist while simultaneously positioning his left hand to grasp uke's elbow (see detail).

2 Tori grips uke's wrist and elbow and exerts a leading and bearing-down pressure. It is important to to draw uke forward slightly to take his balance, and take away his capacity to generate strength in his arm. Then it is a matter of applying your full body weight suddenly and directly on top of the elbow joint.

3 Tori steps back with his leading leg and drops his weight onto uke's arm causing uke to crash to the ground very hard, potentially face first. The technique can be used to restrain the assailant, or if he cannot, or will not, be reasoned with – to incapacitate him as necessary.

Step 1 detail
When tori parries uke's punch, it is not a blocking movement, but a deflection where tori's intent is to stick the back of his hand to uke's wrist/forearm. This movement is used here to facilitate the easy transition of tori's right hand from a parrying position to a position where he can grab uke's wrist.

Defending an Attack with a Weapon from Behind

This technique is an applied version of shomen-uchi irimi-nage. Because this would be a potential life-threatening situation the applications here have to be short, sharp and quick, and not allow uke any time to recover.

1 Tori takes in the tranquil scenery of parkland as uke hovers behind. Uke approaches tori from behind, threatening an overhead strike with a wooden club.

2 Tori turns to face uke and steps in with his left foot while raising his right sword arm to deflect the blow sideways. The contact should never be a full on block using power against power. So here the sword arm (as the sword would be) is held at an angle to deflect the energy of the attack sideways.

3 Tori enters more with his left foot, then turns his body to face in the same direction as the attacker while at the same time cutting the attacking arm down in front of him with his right arm and trapping it against his right side. Tori takes the back of uke's collar and pulls back...

4 ...simultaneously striking him in the face with his right hand and knocking uke backwards (see detail).

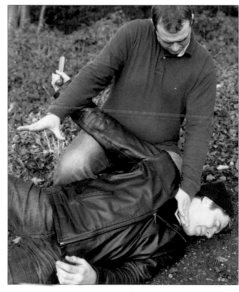

5 Dropping to his left knee, tori controls the weapon-wielding arm by applying strong pressure it with his sword arm. At the same time tori applies pressure with his left handblade against uke's carotid (neck) artery. Do not apply too much pressure on the neck artery, unless uke is still very determined. The idea here is to encourage uke to let go of the weapon.

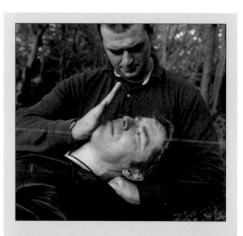

Step 4 detail
In the traditional irimi-nage technique you cut across uke's face/neck as you enter to throw him, giving him a chance to take ukemi or neutralize the attack. Because there is a weapon, it needs to be extracted from uke quickly. This simultaneous pull-back with the left hand and face strike with the other (open hand or fist can be used) disorients uke until he finds himself controlled.

Advanced Throws

As a student progresses and, providing they develop a good understanding of ukemi, more advanced training is available. The pictures here show what is possible at an advanced level within aikido training. Looking at these as a beginner you would be forgiven for thinking that they appear daunting. The reality is, however, that once you have the ability to relax and harmonize with the movement, these throws become relatively easy.

Once again, there is no attitude of conflict within such training, and although the techniques are always practised with full commitment there is also an attitude of harmony between uke and tori. Uke attacks hard but then, as the technique is applied, uke waits for his balance to be taken and then becomes "the other half" of the technique. In this way tori and uke execute natural movements between themselves, tori performing the technique and uke effortlessly flipping over.

Ryote-dori kokyu-nage 1

Above This throw shows a stage before the ryote-dori kokyu-nage, or two-handed grab on two hands breath throw, which is shown on the opposite page. Here tori has just raised his upper body and is about to extend his arms upwards and outwards to complete the movement.

Ryo kube-shime koshi-nage

Above This is a ryote kube-shime koshi-nage, or two-handed choke-attack hip throw. Uke has extended his hands towards tori's neck in an attempt to choke him. Just before uke's hands make contact tori grabs uke's wrists and begins to extend them over his head, bringing uke forward and unbalancing him. Tori then bends his knees, loads uke's body onto his hips and looks in the same direction as uke. Uke rides over tori's hips and flips forward into a natural ukemi. This is given impetus by a rapid reversing of the hips, as tori changes posture from right to left.

Ryote-dori kokyu-nage 2

Right This throw, called ryote-dori kokyu-nage or two-handed grab on two hands breath throw, involves uke attacking from the front and grabbing both of tori's wrists. Tori raises both hands simultaneously and drops his head and shoulders under uke's waist in front of his upper thigh. By harmonizing with uke's forward motion tori raises his upper body sharply and flips uke high into the air overhead. Tori also spreads his arms to add impetus to the throw and ensure that uke rides over his left or right shoulder.

Kokyu-nage

Juji garami-nage

Right This technique is known as juji garami-nage, or crossed-arm twining throw. Uke has grabbed both of tori's wrists from behind (ushiro). Tori at first steps back with his right foot and then immediately back again and at the same time draws uke's arms over his head, capturing both of uke's wrists with a grip of his own. Then tori wraps uke's right arm over his left and exerts strong pressure against the joints. Tori enters and, with a hip turn, throws uke as shown. It is important to let go of uke's forward arm as depicted here. This is to enable uke to take ukemi properly and not be injured.

Ganseki otoshi

Above This is another example of kokyu-nage or breath throw. Here uke has attempted to punch tori in the face with her right fist (jodan tsuki, or upper thrust). Tori has stepped in with his rear foot, lowering and turning his body inwards to avoid the attack and has come up from underneath with a large sweeping movement of both arms. This, combined with a strong hip turn flips uke over tori's leading leg.

Right This is a variation of irimi-nage called ganseki otoshi, or head-over-heels throw, and involves uke rolling over tori. As with all aikido techniques uke's safety is of paramount importance. So although this picture shows uke in a very vulnerable situation, the reality is that he is literally placed on his feet by tori and so is never in any real danger. This is an extremely exhilarating technique to practise as long as both uke and tori have complete confidence in one another.

Styles of Aikido

There is only one traditional aikido and that is the art created by and disseminated by its founder, Morihei Ueshiba. This tradition is carried on today by the headquarters of the Aikikai Foundation (also called Hombu Dojo or Hombu) led by the founder's grandson, Moriteru Ueshiba, the aikido doshu, or "master of the way", and by the remaining uchideshi, who are teaching all over the world. Throughout its history aikido has seen many colourful characters, people who have contributed immensely to the art's diverse development. Minoru Mochizuki (1907–2003) was a student of judo's founder, Kano Jigoro, and was despatched by Kano to study with Morihei Ueshiba in 1930. In 1931, Mochizuki opened the Yoseikan dojo to establish a composite martial art combining elements of aikido, judo, kendo and, later, karate.

Another notable judoka was sent by Kano Jigoro to train with Morihei Ueshiba around the same time. Professor Kenji Tomiki (1900–79) had met the aikido founder in 1926 and was

Above The late Yamaguchi Seigo 8th Dan Shihan, one of the most influential teachers from Hombu Dojo, teaching at a seminar in Oxford, England.

greatly impressed by him. In 1940 Ueshiba awarded him Menkyo Kaiden, a certifying document that roughly equates to 8th Dan. He was the first aikido student to reach this level. He went on to amalgamate elements of his judo skills with aikido and created tomiki, or sport aikido. Competition is involved here with the use of rubber

knives and a points system that Kenji Tomiki believed would sharpen reflexes and make aikido more combat oriented. Gozo Shioda (1915–74) started aikido training in 1932. He established the yoshinkan style of aikido, characterized by short, sharp movements and the positive application of joint techniques. The world headquarters for yoshinkan aikido is in the same district of Tokyo as the Aikikai Foundation.

Koichi Tohei (b. 1920) is the only person to be officially awarded 10th Dan by the Hombu (1970). A year or so later he attempted to establish his teaching methods at Hombu, but was rejected, which ultimately led to his resignation from the Aikikai in 1974. He went on to establish the shin shin toitsu style, which places great emphasis on the development of ki. There are many great teachers of aikido who, although prior students of the founder, have gone on to create new branches of the art. Most follow the founder's way, though some do not – such is the nature of the art and the individual interpretation of its ideals.

Finding a Club

Above Chiba Sensei 8th Dan Shihan with the author in Bridgenorth, England in 1987. Chiba Sensei was the Aikikai Hombu official delegate to Great Britain.

There is a lot of choice when looking for a suitable club. When looking for a dojo, make a shortlist of clubs in the your area that are officially recognized by a nationally accredited organization, and make sure that this organization is a member of the relevant aikido authority. Only then are you certain of the quality and service that you should expect. A club should insist that everyone is individually insured, as it is possible that your policy could be invalidated if the person you are training with is injured and has no cover. It is now a ruling in Great Britain that an instructor teaching students up to the age of 18 has to have a children's coaching award, too.

The organizations referred to opposite all represent Aikikai Hombu style traditional aikido, although some of them also act on behalf of other styles of aikido. Some countries have an umbrella body to regulate the member associations, whereas associations in other countries have full authority from that country's government to do whatever is necessary for the legitimate advancement of aikido. There are countless more clubs and groups of clubs outside any recognized authority in every country of the world. For peace of mind you are advised to look for a club that operates under the auspices of a recognized association or federation, for if you are injured or suffer some other misfortune you can look forward to their full support for a (in most cases) negligible fee.

AUSTRALIA
Shihan Seiichi Sugano, the Hombu representative to Australia established the Aikikai of Australia in 1964. They have authority from the federal government under the national coaching accreditation scheme to issue guidelines for the advancement of aikido for insurance, grading requirements and coaching qualifications.

CANADA
The Canadian Aikido Federation acts both as an insurance agent for the membership of an affiliated organization and also has a function as an umbrella body to other groups.

FRANCE
The Ministry of Youth and Sports in France recognizes the Union of Federations of Aikido of which the two Hombu recognized groups are the FFAAA headed by Christian Tissier Shihan and the FFAB lead by Nobuyoshi Tamura Shihan.

GERMANY
Aikido organizations in Germany include the Deutscher Judo Bund (DJB) with 1,500 aikidoka as members; the Deutscher Aikido Bund (DAB), the largest group with an enrolment of more than 4,500 practitioners; the German Aikikai with some 3,400 members; and the Freie Deutsche Aikido Vereinigung (FDAV), with about 300 members.

GREECE
Aikido organizations in Greece register through the Ministry of Culture and Sports and newly formed groups have to register with a lawyer.

Above Photograph taken in 1974 at the Philbeach Gardens Dojo in Earls Court, London. Back row from left: the author, Phillip Smith, Alwyn Joseph, David Jones, Graham Thomas, the late Marian Mucha, Terry Kenny; front row from left: Gordon Jones, Chiba Sensei, William Smith.

NEW ZEALAND
The New Zealand Aikikai is headed by Takase Shihan. This group is recognized by the government and has full authority to establish aikido guidelines.

SOUTH AFRICA
The South African Sports Confederation and Olympic Committee is the organization to which the Martial Arts Authority of South Africa is affiliated. Subordinate to that is the Aikido Federation of South Africa (AFSA), a Hombu recognized organization and a member of The International Aikido Federation.

SPAIN
Here, aikido is incorporated into a Judo federation called Diciplina Associada. This issues teaching certificates that are recognized by the government. However, because of the lack of a Hombu shihan in the organization many individuals affiliate to associations fronted by Tamura Sensei, Kitaura Sensei, Yamada Sensei and Endo Sensei.

UK
Aikido comes under the British Aikido Board (BAB), set up to oversee all styles of aikido and their development in terms of safety, behaviour and coaching. An instructor's qualification is ratified with the ascending categories of coach levels 1, 2 and 3 and coach tutor, rankings awarded only after rigorous testing. BAB. is working towards creating a system that will replace these and culminate in a National Vocational Qualification (NVQ) in aikido. It also acts as an insurance agent and looks after the implementation of any government or EU-driven policy changes.

USA
Hombu affiliated organizations in the USA register with the United States Aikido Federation (USAF), split into four regions: Eastern, Midwestern, Western and Latin American. Technical issues, grading requirements and the issuing of teaching licences are the responsibility of the Hombu shihan in charge of the respective region.

Useful Contacts

THE AIKIKAI FOUNDATION

The headquarters of the Aikikai Foundation is the Aikikai-So-Hombu, Tokyo, Japan. The chairman is the founder's grandson, Moriteru Ueshiba, the world leader of traditional aikido with a mission to preserve the teachings of Ueshiba. Referred to as Hombu Dojo, the building is built on the same site as the original wooden structure Kobukan dojo created in 1932. People come from all over the world to train at the Hombu with the doshu and the professional shihan who teach there. The Foundation was commissioned in 1948 and now has more than 50 countries under its wing, all of which follow the rules and regulations laid down by the Foundation. All dojos affiliated to Hombu observe the same etiquette, and dan gradings issued worldwide are awarded. It is recognition by the Aikikai Foundation and the Ueshiba name that are magnets for many aikidokas (students) throughout the world.

Right Yamada Shihan, 8th Dan. Aikikai delegate to USA, Cardiff National Sports Centre, 1985, throwing the author with tenchi-nage, or heaven and earth throw.

THE INTERNATIONAL AIKIDO FEDERATION

As the popularity of aikido spread, there was a need for an official body to monitor and oversee this growth and to ensure that the national organizations that were officially recognized by the Aikikai Foundation could voice their opinions and needs on the international scene. In 1976 the International Aikido Federation (IAF) was created. The head of this organization is always the doshu, in his capacity as the world leader of aikido, and further consists of appointed delegates from each organization representing its respective country.

The IAF meets together in the form of a congress every four years at various locations around the world to discuss all matters relevant to aikido. There is usually a training course laid on to run concurrently to enable representatives from around the world to train together under the instruction of some of the world's top shihan. Decisions are made at these congress sessions by a process of democratic voting and results are ratified by a body known as the Superior Council, whose members are appointed to ensure that the traditional values of aikido, as taught by the founder, are adhered to. Another function of the congress is to elect officials to manage the IAF. These officials come under the auspices of another appointed body, the directing committee, which meets every two years to discuss items of less importance and are subordinate to the IAF congress. Currently, there are 43 aikido organizations worldwide that are members of the International Aikido Federation.

Left The author with Moriteru Ueshiba, grandson of the founder, Hombu Dojo, Tokyo, Japan, 2003.

THE AIKIKAI FOUNDATION

Aikido World Headquarters
17–18 Wakamatsu Cho, Shinjuku-ku,
Tokyo, 162÷0056 Japan
Tel: (+81) 3-3203-9236
aikido@aikikai.or.jp

THE INTERNATIONAL AIKIDO FEDERATION

Address as the Aikikai Foundation, above.
general.secretary@aikido-international.org
www.aikido-international.org

AUSTRALIA

MAKOTOKAN BUDO
Castle Hill, Sydney, NSW
Tel: +61 2 9639 7838

QUEENSLAND AIKIDO CENTRE
1/2 Sunlight Drive, Burleigh West
Gold Coast
Tel: +61 7 5559 5483; www.qld.aikido.org.au

CANADA

CALGARY AIKIKAI
507 36 Ave SE, Calgary, Alberta T2G 1W5
Tel: +1 403 243 9880
www.calgaryaikikai.com
info@calgaryaikikai.com

JCCC AIKIKAI
c/o Japanese Canadian Cultural Centre
6 Garamond Court
Toronto, Ontario M3C 1Z5
Tel: +1 416 441 2345; www.jcccaikikai.ca

VANCOUVER WEST AIKIKAI
Kitsilano Community Centre
2690 Larch St., Vancouver, B.C. VDK
Tel: +1 604 222 2211
www.vancouverwestaikikai.com

FRANCE
FFAB
c/o Fédération Française d'Aïkido et de
Budo, Les Allées, 83149 Bras
Tel: +33 4 98 05 22 28
Anne Vovan at nfo@aikido-paris-idf.org

GERMANY
AIKIKAI OF GERMANY
Aikido-Schule Charlottenstrasse
Charlottenstrasse 26–28, Hamburg 20257
Tel: +49 40 4327 1913
info@aikido-schule-charlottenstrasse.de

GREECE
THE HELLENIC AIKIDO ASSOCIATION
FukiShinKan Dojo, 144 Athens GR112 51
Tel: +30 210 881 1768; aikidogr@acci.gr

S.C. ATRAPOS
Yudokan Kojo, 12 Vlaxernon Str.
551 33 Vizantio, Thessaloniki
Tel: +30 231 048 0089;
aikido@atrapos.gr

NEW ZEALAND
AUCKLAND RIAI AIKIDO
Ponsonby Communty Centre, 20
Ponsonby Terrace, Ponsonby
Tel: +64 9 444 0921;
auckland.info@aikido.org.nz

SOUTH AFRICA
AFSA, c/o Aikido Federation of South
Africa; P O Box 1182, Heidelburg 1438
Tel: +27 11 744 0009; aikido@mweb.co.za

SPAIN
ASSOCIACION CULTURAL FEILEN AIKIDO
Dojo Central c/Liuva, 39 Bajos 08030,
Sant Andreu, Barcelona
Tel: +34 655 88 95 92; aikifeilen@aikifeilen.com

UK
THE BRITISH AIKIDO BOARD (BAB)
General Secretary, 6 Halkingcroft,
Langley, Slough, Berkshire SL3 7AT;
john.burn@clara.co.uk

USA
AIKIDO SCHOOLS OF UESHIBA
29165 Singletary Road
Myakka City, FL 34251; Tel: +1 941 322-1252

BERKELEY AIKIKAI
1812 San Pablo Avenue
Berkeley, CA 94702; Tel: +1 510 549 1518

HIDEKI SHIOHIRA
2531 Titan Way, Castro Valley CA 94546
Tel: +1 510 481 1734

Above The late Saito Morihiro 9th Dan Shihan, in Cambridge, England, 1989.

NEW YORK AIKIKAI
142 W. 18th Street, New York NY 10011
Tel: +1 212 242 6246;
secretary@nyaikikai.com

SAN DIEGO AIKIKAI
3844 Adams Avenue, San Diego CA 92116
Tel: +1 619 280 7059
sdaikikai@aol.com

INTERNET SITES
www.aikidojournal.com
www.aikidofaq.com
www.aiki.com
www.aikiweb.com
www.aikido-world.com
www.britishaikikai.co.uk
www.ukaonline.co.uk

Further Reading

Dang, Phong Thong, *Aikido Basics*, Tuttle Publishing, 2003
Pranin, Stanley, *The Aiki News Encyclopedia*, Aiki News, 1989.
Stevens, John, *The Essence of Aikido*, Kodansha, 1999
Strozzi Heckler, Richard, *Aikido and the New Warrior*, North Atlantic Books, 1985
Ueshiba, Kisshomaru, *The Spirit of Aikido*, Kodansha International, 1987
Ueshiba, Kisshomaru and Moriteru, *Best Aikido: The Fundamentals,* Kodansha International, 2002 Ueshiba, Morihei, Kodansha International, 1993

Ueshiba, Morihei, *Budo: Teachings of the Founder of Aikido*, Kodansha International, 1991
Ueshiba, Moriteru, *The Aikido Master Course*, (Best Aikido 2), Kodansha International, 2003
Westbrook, A., and Ratti, O., *Aikido and the Dynamic Sphere*, Tuttle Publishing, 1970
Yamada, Yoshimitsu, *The New Aikido Complete: The Arts of Power and Movement*, Lyle Stuart, 1981

Glossary

Ai	Harmony
Ai hanmi	Same or matched stance
Aiki	Blended or matched ki
Aiki jo	Staff or stick used in aikido
Aiki ken	Aikido swordmanship
Aiki-nage	Aiki throw
Aiki otoshi	Aiki drop
Aiki taiso	Aiki exercises
Ashi	Foot
Ashi sabaki	Footwork
Atemi	Strike or blow
Awase	Blending movement
Ayumi ashi	Walking
Batto	Sword drawing
Bo	Stick larger than a jo
Bojutsu	Stick techniques
Bokken	Wooden sword
Bokuto	Wooden sword (also bokken)
Budo	Martial way
Budoka	Martial artist
Bujutsu	Martial technique
Bukidori	Against arms
Bukiwaza	Weapons techniques
Chikara no dashikata	The extension of power
Chudan kamae	Middle stance
Dakishime	Hug
Do	Way, path
Dogi	Practice suit (also gi, keikogi)
Dojo	Training hall
Doshu	Leader of the way
Eri dori	Collar or lapel grab
Fuku shidoin	Assistant instructor
Futaridori	Attack by two opponents
Futarigake	Attack by two opponents
Gedan	Lower
Gi	Practice suit (also keikogi, dogi)
Gokkyo	Wrist pin
Gyaku	Reverse, opposite
Gyaku hanmi	Reverse or opposite stance
Haishin undo	After-practice back-bending exercise
Hakama	Pleated skirt
Hanmi	Half stance (also kamae)
Hanmi handachi	One standing, one sitting
Hara	Stomach, abdomen
Henka waza	Variation technique
Hidari	Left
Hito e mi	Stance (oblique hanmi)
Ho	Exercise, method
Ikkyo	Arm pin
Irimi	Entering movement
Irimi-nage	Entering throw
Jo	Short staff
Jodan	Upper position
Jodan no kamae	Upper stance with sword
Jodo	Art of the jo
Ju no keiko	Practise softly
Ju no ri	Principle of gentleness
Jumbi taiso	Warm-up exercises
Jyugeuko	Free practice
Jyugi	Free attack and defence
Jyuwaza	Free attack and defence
Kaiten ashi	Forward-step pivot
Kaiten-nage	Rotary throw
Kamae	Postures for combat
Kansetsu	Joint
Kansetsu waza	Joint technique
Kata (1)	Form
Kata (2)	Shoulder

Kata-dori	Shoulder grab
Katame waza	Immobilization technique
Katana	Long sword
Katate	One hand
Katate-dori	One-hand grab
Katatori	Shoulder grab (kata-dori)
Keiko	Practice, training
Keikogi	Practice suit (also gi, dogi)
Kekka fusi	Sitting position
Ken dori	Against sword
Ki	Spirit
Kiai	Combative shout
Kiritsu	Standing/stand
Kodachi	Short sword
Kogeki	Attack
Koho tento	Falling backward
Kokoro	Spirit, heart
Kokyu	Breath
Kokyu-ho	Breathing method
Kokyu-nage	Breath throw
Kokyu no henka	Breath changes
Kokyu-ryoku	Breath power (kokyu)
Kokyu tenkan ho	Breath turning
Koshi-nage	Hip throw
Kote-gaeshi	Wrist out turn or twist
Kote hineri	Wrist twist, sankyo
Kote mawashi	Wrist in turn, nikkyo
Kubi	Neck
Kubi shime	Choke, strangle
Kyu	Class, grade below shodan
Mawatte	Turn
Ma-ai	Distance between opponents
Men	Head
Menuchi	Head strike
Metsuke	Eye-to-eye contact
Migi	Right
Mochi	Hold, grasp
Morote-dori	Two-hand grab
Mune-dori	Chest hold
Nage	Throw
Neko ashi dachi	Cat stance
Nikkyo	Control wrist by turning in
Nori	Attention stand
Omote	Front
Oyowaza	Applied techniques
Randori	Free-style practice
Rei	Bow

Renoji dachi	Stance "l"
Renshu	Practice, training
Renzoku	Continuous
Ritsurei	Standing bow
Rokkyo	Elbow pin
Ryokata-dori	Two-shoulder grab
Ryote-dori	Two-hand grab
Ryu	Style, school
Sabaki	Movement
Sankaku	Triangle
Sankyo	Control wrist by twisting it
Sannindori	Attack by three opponents
Seiza	Seated position
Sensei	Teacher
Shidoin	Instructor
Shihan	Master instructor
Shiho-nage	Four-corner throw
Shikko	Samurai knee walking
Shisei	Posture
Shomen-uchi	Front-head strike
Shumatsu dosa	After-practice back-bending exercise
Sode	Sleeve
Sode-dori	Sleeve grab
Sotai dosa	Paired exercise
Suburi	Exercise for jo and bokken
Sumi	Corner
Sumi otoshi	Corner drop
Suwariwaza	Seated techniques
Tachi	Standing
Tachidori	Sword taking
Tachiwaza	Standing techniques
Tai	Body
Taijutsu	Body techniques (unarmed)
Tanden	Centre of stomach, or gravity
Tandoku dosa	Solo exercises
Tandoku keiko	Practise by oneself
Taninzudori	Attack by many opponents
Tanken	Knife
Tanken dori	Knife-defence action
Tanto	Knife
Tanto dori	Knife-defence action
Tatami	Straw practice mat
Te Sabaki	Hand movement
Tegatana	Hand blade
Teiji dachi	Stance "t"
Tekubi	Wrist
Tekubi osae	Wrist pin, yonkyo
Tenchi-nage	Heaven and earth throw
Tenkan	Turn
Tenkan ashi	Pivot
Tsugi ashi	Following steps, shuffle step
Tsuki	Punch
Uchi	Strike
Uchideshi	Live-in student
Ude	Arm
Ude-hishigi	Arm smashing
Ude-nobashi	Arm stretch
Uke	One who receives
Ukemi	The art of falling
Ura	Back
Ushiro	Rear, behind
Waza	Technique
Yame	Stop, finish or end
Yoko	Side
Yokomen	Side of the head
Yokomen-uchi	Strike to the side of the head
Yonkyo	Inner forearm nerve pinch
Yudansha	Black-belt student
Za ho	Sitting method
Zarei	Formal sitting bow

Index

Acknowledgements

PUBLISHER'S ACKNOWLEDGEMENTS

The publisher would like to thank the following for the use of their pictures in the book (l=left, r=right, t=top, b=bottom, m=middle): p6, p7l, p7r, p18; p29b, p122t, p122b, p123, p124t, p124b, p125, p128 Peter Brady; p11tl, p11tr Mary Evans Picture Library; p11b Jesper Hoejdal; p19t Michael Riehle; p19b Herman Kempers; p20tl Karen Wolek; p20tr Daniel Kestenholz; p23b Tammy Lee Anderson (Shinzen Dojo, Clovis, California, www.healing-wellness.com); p113 Rex Features.

All other photographs © Anness Publishing Ltd

Every effort has been made to find the copyright holders and acknowledge the pictures properly; however we apologize if there are any unintentional omissions, which will be corrected in future editions.

AUTHOR'S ACKNOWLEDGEMENTS

First of all I would like to thank the aikido founder, the late Morihei Ueshiba, for enriching the world with his vision of peace and harmony.

I would also like to thank T. K. Chiba Shihan, for his inspiration, not just in his unsurpassed technical ability in both aikido body art and weapons but in his commitment and dedication to the art itself.

I owe a debt of gratitude to Nobuyoshi Tamura Shihan, head of aikido in France, for his warmth and friendly advice over the years and to Yoshimitsu Yamada from America for his help and guidance. There are many more, too numerous to mention individually, who have helped to shape my aikido development – to those I am forever grateful.

To Shihan W. J. Smith MBE, founder of the United Kingdom Aikikai, a heartfelt thank you for a lifetime's support, friendship and lessons in how to be a true gentleman of aikido. Thanks also to my fellow shidoin (teachers) at the UKA for supporting each other and being there for one another. The organization would not be what it is today without them being the people they are.

Thanks to photographer Mike James for his skill and good-humoured professionalism and to my editor Emma Clegg for taking on the project and following through so well.

To my students, too, a big thank you for your encouragement and enthusiasm. A particular mention to the students who assisted me as models in the photography: Cliff Price, Cath Davies, Paul Jarvis, Eddie McCalla, Kelly Magna, Neil Mould, Bryn Ross, Richard Hughes, Kevin Beggan, Rivington Hermitt, Debbie Shadbolt and, last but by no means least, my children Charlotte, James and Jonathan.

Finally, a very special thanks to all my family who have on many occasions had to tolerate my being up all hours of the day and night to get this project finished!

Left The author with friend and mentor W. J. Smith 6th Dan Shihan, 2005